GUARDIANS OF THE DIGITAL FRONTIER

Advanced Strategies in Data Science and Intelligent Decision Systems

Uzochukwu Edwin Nwobi

Contents

Preface

Digital systems now form the backbone of decision making across industries, governments, and research institutions. From financial risk analysis and security monitoring to healthcare diagnostics and operational planning, data driven intelligence has become inseparable from how modern systems function. As these systems grow more complex, the responsibility placed on data science and artificial intelligence practitioners has expanded beyond technical execution into areas of trust, resilience, and long term impact.

This book was conceived in response to that shift. *Guardians of the Digital Frontier: Advanced Strategies in Data Science and Intelligent Decision Systems* is designed as an advanced, research focused contribution that examines how intelligent systems should be built, evaluated, and sustained in environments where accuracy alone is not sufficient. The emphasis of this work is not only on innovation, but on the disciplined application of data science methodologies that can withstand operational pressure, ethical scrutiny, and evolving real world conditions.

Over the past decade, data science literature has grown rapidly, often highlighting breakthroughs in algorithms, model performance, and computational efficiency. While these advances are essential, they represent only part of the equation. Intelligent systems exist within broader ecosystems that include data governance structures, human oversight, regulatory expectations, and infrastructural constraints. This book addresses that broader context by treating data science as a systems level discipline rather than a collection of isolated techniques.

The motivation behind this work is rooted in the observation that many analytical systems fail not because the underlying models are weak, but because they are poorly integrated, insufficiently governed, or inadequately optimized for long term use. Decisions driven by data carry real consequences, and errors in analytical judgment can propagate quickly when systems scale. For this reason, the book places strong emphasis on integrity, accountability, and resilience as core pillars of intelligent decision system design.

Each chapter engages deeply with advanced methodologies in data science, machine learning, and artificial intelligence, while also addressing how these methods interact with operational realities. Topics such as model lifecycle management, governance frameworks, analytical robustness, and risk aware optimization are explored in detail. The discussions are supported by peer reviewed research, academic references, and established theoretical foundations, ensuring that the work maintains strong scholarly value alongside practical relevance.

The structure of the book reflects a deliberate progression. Foundational concepts are revisited at an advanced level, followed by detailed examinations of algorithmic intelligence, system architecture, and decision frameworks. Later chapters expand into resilience, governance, and future facing innovations, offering readers a comprehensive view of how intelligent systems evolve over time. This approach allows the book to function both as a reference for experienced professionals and as a structured guide for advanced academic study.

This work is intended for readers who already possess a working knowledge of data science and artificial intelligence. It is written for researchers, advanced practitioners, graduate level students, and professionals responsible for designing, evaluating, or overseeing intelligent decision systems. While the material is rigorous, it is also presented with the aim of clarity, encouraging readers to think critically about both the technical and ethical dimensions of their work.

At its core, this book is about responsibility in the digital age. As intelligent systems increasingly influence economic stability, security outcomes, and societal processes, those who design and manage them occupy positions of significant trust. Being a guardian of the digital frontier means recognizing that innovation must be matched with discipline, foresight, and accountability. This book is offered as a guide and a reference for those who accept that responsibility and seek to build intelligent systems that are not only powerful, but dependable, transparent, and aligned with long term human interests.

Foreword

The expansion of data science and artificial intelligence has fundamentally reshaped how modern systems reason, predict, and decide. Across sectors such as finance, security, healthcare, governance, and enterprise operations, intelligent systems now influence outcomes that carry economic, social, and ethical weight. As these systems grow in scale and autonomy, the question facing practitioners and researchers is no longer whether data driven intelligence is powerful, but whether it is being designed and managed with sufficient rigor, responsibility, and foresight.

This book speaks directly to that challenge. *Guardians of the Digital Frontier: Advanced Strategies in Data Science and Intelligent Decision Systems* is a serious and carefully constructed contribution that addresses the maturity phase of data science as a discipline. It moves beyond introductory explanations and surface level innovation narratives to focus on how intelligent systems should function when accuracy, resilience, and trust are non negotiable requirements.

One of the strengths of this work lies in its recognition that intelligent decision systems do not operate in isolation. Models are embedded within infrastructures, governed by organizational processes, shaped by data quality, and interpreted by human decision makers. Failures in these systems often emerge not from algorithmic weakness alone, but from poor integration, insufficient oversight, or a lack of accountability across the analytical lifecycle.

This book acknowledges those realities and addresses them directly through a systems oriented and research grounded approach.

The chapters that follow demonstrate a thoughtful balance between theory and application. Advanced data science methodologies and machine learning strategies are presented alongside discussions of governance, optimization, and operational integrity. Rather than treating these topics as peripheral concerns, the author positions them as essential components of intelligent system design. This perspective reflects an understanding that innovation without structure can quickly become a liability when systems scale or operate under pressure.

From a scholarly standpoint, the work is well anchored in established research. The use of peer reviewed literature and academic references strengthens its credibility and positions the book as a valuable resource for advanced study. At the same time, the writing remains attentive to practical relevance. The concepts discussed are clearly connected to real world decision environments, making the book useful not only to researchers, but also to professionals responsible for deploying and supervising intelligent systems.

Another notable aspect of this book is its attention to stewardship and leadership in data driven environments. As intelligent systems increasingly support or automate decisions, the role of human judgment becomes more nuanced rather than obsolete. This work reinforces the importance of interpretability, ethical awareness, and governance frameworks that ensure intelligence remains aligned with human values and institutional responsibility. Such considerations are especially critical in high impact domains where errors can propagate quickly and at scale.

This book is particularly well suited for advanced practitioners, graduate level students, researchers, and technical leaders who are already familiar with core data science concepts and seek deeper engagement with the discipline. It challenges readers to think critically about how intelligent systems are built, evaluated, and sustained over time. In doing so, it encourages a mindset that values durability, transparency, and accountability alongside innovation.

As the digital frontier continues to expand, those who design and manage intelligent systems assume a role that extends beyond technical problem solving. They become stewards of systems that influence trust, stability, and decision quality across society. This book offers a thoughtful and comprehensive guide for those willing to take that responsibility seriously. It is a timely contribution to the field and a meaningful reference for anyone committed to advancing data science and intelligent decision systems with discipline and purpose.

Introduction

The modern digital landscape is defined by an unprecedented reliance on data driven intelligence. Across industries, institutions, and societies, decisions that once depended solely on human experience are now shaped by analytical models, predictive systems, and algorithmic reasoning. Data science and intelligent decision systems have become central to how organizations assess risk, allocate resources, anticipate outcomes, and respond to uncertainty. This shift represents not just a technological evolution, but a fundamental change in how knowledge is produced and applied.

As computational capabilities have expanded, so has the ambition of intelligent systems. Early analytical tools focused primarily on descriptive reporting and retrospective analysis. Today, advanced data science methodologies enable systems to forecast behavior, optimize performance, and automate complex decisions in real time. Machine learning and artificial intelligence now operate within critical environments such as finance, cybersecurity, healthcare, logistics, and governance, where accuracy, reliability, and accountability are essential rather than optional.

Yet alongside these advancements lies a growing tension. Many intelligent systems achieve impressive performance in controlled or experimental settings but encounter limitations when deployed at scale. Data drift, biased inputs, opaque decision logic, and weak governance structures can undermine even the most sophisticated models. These challenges reveal an important truth: intelligence that is technically advanced but structurally fragile can introduce new forms of risk. The effectiveness of data driven decision systems therefore depends not only on innovation, but on disciplined design and responsible oversight.

This book is grounded in that understanding. *Guardians of the Digital Frontier: Advanced Strategies in Data Science and Intelligent Decision Systems* examines how data science and artificial intelligence can be applied in ways that support dependable, transparent, and resilient decision making. Rather than focusing narrowly on algorithms, the book explores the full lifecycle of intelligent systems, from data collection and model development to deployment, governance, and long term maintenance. In doing so, it presents data science as an integrated discipline that operates within technical, organizational, and ethical boundaries.

A key premise of this work is that intelligent systems exist within complex ecosystems. Data pipelines, computational infrastructure, regulatory requirements, and human decision makers all influence how intelligence is produced and interpreted. Effective systems must therefore account for these interacting components. This book addresses that complexity by emphasizing analytical integrity, system resilience, and governance as foundational elements of intelligent decision frameworks.

The chapters that follow engage deeply with advanced data science methodologies and machine learning strategies, while also addressing how these methods perform under real operational conditions. Topics such as model optimization, performance stability, anomaly detection, and risk analytics are explored alongside discussions of accountability, transparency, and oversight. Each chapter is supported by peer reviewed research and academic references, reinforcing the scholarly foundation of the work and situating it within ongoing research discourse.

Another central theme of this book is the evolving relationship between human judgment and machine intelligence. While automation continues to expand, intelligent systems rarely operate independently of human oversight. Decisions informed by data must still be interpreted, validated, and contextualized by people who understand the broader implications of analytical outcomes. This book emphasizes approaches that preserve human agency while leveraging computational intelligence to enhance clarity and consistency in decision making.

The intended audience for this work includes advanced practitioners, researchers, graduate level students, and technical leaders who already possess foundational knowledge of data science and artificial intelligence. The material assumes familiarity with core concepts and seeks to extend that understanding into areas of system design, governance, and long term sustainability. Readers are encouraged to engage critically with the frameworks presented and to consider how these strategies can be adapted to their own domains.

As intelligent systems continue to shape economic performance, security outcomes, and social processes, the responsibility borne by those who design and manage them becomes increasingly significant. Decisions informed by data can scale rapidly, amplifying both benefits and errors. In this context, data scientists and system architects serve as guardians of a digital frontier where trust, resilience, and accountability must be actively maintained.

This book is offered as a guide for those guardians. It provides a structured exploration of advanced strategies in data science and intelligent decision systems, with the aim of supporting systems that are not only innovative, but dependable and ethically grounded. By integrating technical rigor with stewardship, the work seeks to contribute meaningfully to the future of data driven intelligence in an increasingly complex digital world.

Chapter 1

Foundations of Advanced Data Science in Digital Systems

The evolution of data science has followed the broader trajectory of digital transformation, moving from basic statistical analysis to complex systems capable of learning, adapting, and supporting autonomous decision making. In its early stages, data science focused primarily on descriptive and diagnostic analytics, providing summaries of historical data and explanations of past outcomes. While these approaches offered value, they were limited in scope and impact. Today, data science operates as a foundational pillar of digital systems, shaping how organizations anticipate change, manage uncertainty, and act in real time.

Advanced data science differs from its foundational form not only in technical sophistication, but also in purpose. It is no longer sufficient to generate insights after events have occurred. Modern digital environments demand predictive, prescriptive, and adaptive intelligence that can function continuously within operational systems. This shift has elevated data science from an analytical support role to an embedded system capability, influencing outcomes at scale across finance, security, healthcare, logistics, governance, and enterprise operations.

At the core of advanced data science lies the ability to work with complex data structures. Contemporary systems generate data that is high dimensional, heterogeneous, and often unstructured. Transaction logs, sensor streams, text data, images, and network interactions coexist within the same analytical ecosystems. Managing this complexity requires more than traditional statistical tools. It demands robust data engineering practices, probabilistic reasoning, and computational frameworks capable of handling uncertainty and scale.

One defining characteristic of advanced data science is its reliance on probabilistic thinking rather than deterministic assumptions. Real world data is noisy, incomplete, and subject to change. Models built on rigid assumptions often fail when exposed to shifting conditions. Probabilistic models, Bayesian approaches, and stochastic methods allow systems to represent uncertainty explicitly and update beliefs as new information becomes available. This capability is essential in environments where decisions must be made despite imperfect knowledge.

Another foundational element is feature representation. Raw data rarely holds value in its original form. Advanced data science emphasizes the transformation of data into representations that capture underlying structure and meaning. Feature engineering, representation learning, and dimensionality reduction techniques play a critical role in enabling models to generalize beyond training data. In modern systems, this process is increasingly automated through techniques such as deep learning, but human understanding remains important in guiding model design and interpretation.

Advanced data science also depends heavily on computational infrastructure. As data volumes increase, analytical processes must scale efficiently. Distributed computing frameworks, cloud based architectures, and parallel processing systems have become integral to modern data science workflows. These infrastructures enable models to be trained on massive datasets and deployed across distributed environments, supporting real time inference and continuous learning. Without such infrastructure, even the most sophisticated models remain impractical.

However, technical capability alone does not define advanced data science. The integration of analytical models into digital systems introduces new challenges related to reliability and maintainability. Models must operate within production environments where latency, resource constraints, and system dependencies affect performance. This requires careful consideration of model complexity, deployment strategies, and monitoring mechanisms. A model that performs well in isolation may fail when embedded within a larger system if these factors are ignored.

Model evaluation is therefore a central concern. Traditional metrics such as accuracy or precision provide limited insight into how a model will behave over time. Advanced data science incorporates evaluation strategies that consider robustness, stability, and sensitivity to change. Stress testing models under simulated conditions, monitoring performance drift, and validating outputs against real world outcomes are essential practices. These approaches help ensure that analytical systems remain dependable as environments evolve.

Another critical foundation is data quality management. Advanced models amplify both the strengths and weaknesses of the data they consume. Poor data quality can lead to biased outcomes, unstable predictions, and erosion of trust in analytical systems. Data science at an advanced level requires systematic approaches to data validation, cleaning, lineage tracking, and governance. These practices ensure that data inputs remain consistent, traceable, and suitable for decision making purposes.

Ethical considerations also intersect with foundational data science practices. As analytical systems influence high impact decisions, issues such as bias, fairness, and transparency become unavoidable. Advanced data science recognizes that ethical risks often emerge from data selection, feature design, and evaluation choices rather than from algorithms alone. Addressing these risks requires deliberate methodological choices and ongoing oversight. Ethical awareness is therefore not an external constraint, but an integral component of responsible data science.

The role of human expertise remains significant despite advances in automation. While machine learning systems can identify patterns at scale, human judgment is required to define objectives, interpret results, and assess implications. Advanced data science frameworks emphasize collaboration between human decision makers and intelligent systems. This collaboration allows analytical outputs to be contextualized within organizational goals, regulatory requirements, and societal expectations.

A defining feature of modern digital systems is their interconnected nature. Analytical models rarely operate in isolation. They interact with other systems, share data across boundaries, and influence downstream processes. This interconnectedness introduces dependencies that can magnify errors or propagate unintended consequences. Advanced data science must therefore account for system interactions and feedback loops. Understanding how models influence and are influenced by surrounding systems is essential for maintaining overall stability.

Resilience is another foundational concern. Digital systems are exposed to disruptions ranging from data anomalies and infrastructure failures to adversarial manipulation. Advanced data science incorporates resilience strategies that enable systems to detect, respond to, and recover from such disruptions. Techniques such as anomaly detection, redundancy, and adaptive learning contribute to system robustness. These strategies help ensure that analytical systems continue to function reliably under adverse conditions.

The lifecycle perspective is also central to advanced data science. Models are not static artifacts. They evolve as data changes, objectives shift, and environments develop. Effective data science practices therefore extend beyond initial model development to include continuous monitoring, retraining, and retirement. Lifecycle management ensures that models remain relevant and aligned with current realities. Without such practices, analytical systems risk becoming outdated or misleading.

From an organizational standpoint, advanced data science requires clear governance structures. Decision rights, accountability mechanisms, and documentation standards support transparency and trust. Governance frameworks define how models are approved, deployed, and reviewed. They also provide mechanisms for addressing failures and updating practices in response to new insights. Strong governance does not hinder innovation. Instead, it creates conditions under which innovation can be sustained responsibly.

The foundations of advanced data science also include a commitment to methodological rigor. Reproducibility, validation, and documentation are essential for ensuring that analytical results can be trusted and scrutinized. In research settings, these practices support scientific integrity. In operational environments, they enable audits, compliance, and continuous improvement. Advanced data science treats rigor not as an academic ideal, but as a practical necessity.

Education and skill development play an important role in sustaining advanced data science capabilities. As tools and techniques evolve, practitioners must continually update their knowledge. This includes not only technical skills, but also understanding of governance, ethics, and system design. Organizations that invest in holistic skill development are better positioned to leverage data science effectively and responsibly.

1.1 Socio Technical Alignment in Advanced Data Science Systems

One area that has not yet been fully explored is the socio technical dimension of advanced data science. Intelligent systems do not operate solely as technical artifacts. They exist within social, organizational, and institutional settings that shape how their outputs are interpreted and acted upon. Advanced data science therefore requires alignment between technical design and human structures such as workflows, incentives, decision authority, and organizational culture.

Socio technical alignment refers to the deliberate coordination between analytical systems and the people who rely on them. A model may be statistically sound, computationally efficient, and well optimized, yet still fail if it does not fit the decision context of its users. For example, a predictive system that produces highly accurate outputs but lacks interpretability may be ignored by decision makers who cannot justify its recommendations. Similarly, an automated decision system may generate resistance if it disrupts established responsibilities or undermines professional judgment.

Advanced data science addresses this challenge by embedding human considerations into system design from the outset. This includes understanding who will use the system, how decisions are currently made, and what constraints shape acceptance and trust. Design choices around explainability, interface clarity, confidence thresholds, and escalation mechanisms become just as important as algorithm selection. In this sense, data science becomes a collaborative discipline that integrates technical intelligence with organizational realities.

Another aspect of socio technical alignment is feedback integration. Intelligent systems should not operate as one directional engines that produce outputs without learning from human response. Advanced systems incorporate feedback loops that allow user behavior, overrides, and contextual input to inform model updates. This interaction improves system relevance over time and reinforces a sense of shared responsibility between humans and machines.

Failure to address socio technical factors can lead to silent breakdowns. Systems may technically function while gradually losing influence or being bypassed altogether. Advanced data science treats such outcomes as design failures rather than user shortcomings. By recognizing that intelligence is co produced by machines and humans, practitioners can build systems that are not only accurate, but trusted and sustained.

Case Study: Decision Support Failure in a Large Scale Credit Analytics Platform

A financial services organization deployed an advanced credit risk analytics platform designed to automate loan approval decisions. The system incorporated high dimensional customer data, probabilistic risk scoring, and real time decision logic. In controlled testing, the model demonstrated strong predictive performance and reduced default rates compared to legacy scoring methods.

However, once deployed, adoption by credit officers declined rapidly. Despite the model's accuracy, decision makers frequently overrode system recommendations or reverted to manual assessments. An internal review revealed that while the model produced reliable scores, it failed to explain its reasoning in a way that aligned with regulatory reporting requirements and internal accountability structures. Credit officers were responsible for justifying decisions to auditors and management, yet the system provided limited transparency into how scores were derived.

The issue was not technical failure, but socio technical misalignment. The system optimized predictive accuracy without adequately addressing interpretability and workflow integration. As a result, users perceived it as a risk rather than a support tool. To resolve the issue, the organization redesigned the platform to include explanation layers that highlighted key contributing factors, confidence ranges, and scenario comparisons. Decision workflows were also adjusted to allow human review at specific risk thresholds.

Following these changes, adoption improved significantly. The case illustrates that advanced data science systems must be designed with both analytical rigor and human context in mind. Intelligence that cannot be integrated into real decision processes ultimately fails to deliver value, regardless of its technical sophistication.

1.2 Data Science Maturity and Institutional Readiness

Another dimension that warrants deeper attention is data science maturity within institutions. Advanced data science does not succeed simply because sophisticated models are introduced. It succeeds when organizations possess the structural readiness to support, govern, and evolve intelligent systems over time. Institutional readiness refers to the extent to which an organization has aligned its data practices, leadership expectations, technical infrastructure, and decision culture to support sustained analytical intelligence.

Many organizations adopt advanced data science tools before developing the maturity required to manage them effectively. This often results in fragmented analytics initiatives, duplicated models, and inconsistent decision outcomes. Advanced data science demands coordinated data ownership, clearly defined responsibilities, and a shared understanding of how intelligence should influence decisions. Without these elements, even well designed systems struggle to achieve lasting impact.

Data science maturity manifests across several dimensions. One dimension is data stewardship. Institutions must treat data as a managed asset rather than a byproduct of operations. This includes clear data ownership, quality standards, access controls, and documentation practices. Advanced models rely on consistent and well governed data flows. Weak stewardship introduces instability and erodes confidence in analytical outputs.

Another dimension is leadership alignment. Senior decision makers play a critical role in shaping how data science is perceived and used. When leadership treats analytics as an experimental function rather than a strategic capability, systems remain peripheral. Advanced data science requires leadership commitment to evidence based decision making, clear sponsorship of analytical initiatives, and willingness to adapt processes in response to analytical insight.

Technical readiness also defines maturity. Advanced data science depends on scalable infrastructure, reliable data pipelines, and deployment environments that support continuous learning. Organizations that lack these capabilities often struggle to move beyond pilot projects. Models may perform well in development settings but fail to integrate into production systems. Institutional readiness ensures that technical innovation is supported by operational stability.

Equally important is decision culture. Advanced data science thrives in environments where analytical outputs are respected, questioned constructively, and incorporated into decision processes. When organizational culture favors intuition over evidence, intelligent systems are sidelined. Maturity involves cultivating a culture where data informs judgment without replacing accountability.

Institutional readiness is not static. It evolves through deliberate investment, learning, and governance refinement. Advanced data science practitioners must therefore engage not only with technical problems but also with organizational change. Building intelligent systems often requires reshaping processes, redefining roles, and establishing new norms around data use.

Case Study: Analytics Maturity Gaps in a Public Sector Decision System

A national public sector agency sought to introduce an advanced analytics platform to improve resource allocation and service delivery. The system incorporated machine learning models designed to forecast demand patterns and optimize operational planning. Initial results from pilot studies showed strong predictive accuracy and clear potential for efficiency gains.

Despite these promising results, the system failed to gain traction once deployed. Operational teams continued to rely on manual planning methods, and analytical recommendations were rarely implemented. An evaluation revealed several institutional readiness gaps. Data ownership was fragmented across departments, leading to inconsistent inputs. There was no centralized governance body responsible for approving or monitoring analytical models. Decision makers lacked clarity on how analytical outputs should be weighed against political and operational considerations.

In addition, the technical infrastructure supporting the system was insufficient for continuous operation. Data pipelines were unstable, and model updates required manual intervention. These limitations created delays and reduced confidence in system outputs. Users perceived the platform as unreliable, even though the underlying models were sound.

To address these issues, the agency initiated a broader data maturity program. A central analytics governance unit was established to oversee data standards, model approval, and performance monitoring. Data ownership roles were clarified, and infrastructure investments were made to stabilize data pipelines. Training programs were introduced to help decision makers interpret and apply analytical outputs responsibly.

Over time, the system became an integrated part of planning processes. The case demonstrates that advanced data science effectiveness depends as much on institutional readiness as on technical innovation. Without maturity across governance, infrastructure, and culture, intelligent systems struggle to move beyond experimentation. With readiness in place, they can become durable assets that support consistent and accountable decision making.

Chapter 2

Machine Learning Architectures and Algorithmic Intelligence

Machine learning has become one of the most influential forces shaping modern data driven systems. What began as a collection of pattern recognition techniques has evolved into a broad set of architectures capable of learning from data, adapting to change, and supporting complex decision processes. In advanced digital environments, machine learning is no longer an experimental tool but a core component of operational intelligence, embedded within systems that function continuously and at scale.

At the heart of machine learning lies the concept of learning from experience. Unlike rule based systems that rely on explicitly programmed logic, machine learning models infer patterns and relationships directly from data. This ability allows systems to operate in environments where rules are incomplete, ambiguous, or constantly evolving. As data volumes grow and decision contexts become more complex, this adaptive capacity becomes increasingly valuable.

Machine learning architectures can be broadly understood through their learning paradigms. Supervised learning focuses on learning mappings between inputs and known outputs, using labeled data to guide model training. This approach underpins many applications such as classification, regression, and forecasting. In advanced systems, supervised models are often used for risk scoring, demand prediction, and anomaly classification, where historical outcomes provide a reference for future decisions.

Unsupervised learning, by contrast, operates without labeled outcomes. Models identify structure within data by detecting clusters, latent variables, or statistical regularities. This paradigm is particularly useful in exploratory analysis, segmentation, and novelty detection. In intelligent systems, unsupervised learning often supports early signal discovery, helping organizations identify emerging patterns before they are fully understood.

Reinforcement learning introduces a different architectural logic. Rather than learning from static datasets, reinforcement learning models learn through interaction with an environment. Actions are evaluated based on rewards or penalties, allowing systems to optimize behavior over time. This approach is especially relevant in dynamic decision environments such as resource allocation, automated control, and sequential decision making, where outcomes depend on a series of interdependent choices.

Beyond learning paradigms, architectural design plays a critical role in machine learning effectiveness. Traditional models such as linear regression, decision trees, and support vector machines remain valuable due to their interpretability and efficiency.

However, many modern applications require more expressive architectures capable of capturing complex nonlinear relationships. Neural networks, and particularly deep learning models, have become central to this shift.

Deep learning architectures enable representation learning, allowing systems to automatically discover features from raw data. Convolutional neural networks excel in processing spatial data such as images and sensor inputs. Recurrent neural networks and their variants support sequential data analysis, making them suitable for time series and language processing. More recently, attention based architectures have transformed how models handle long range dependencies, enabling more flexible and scalable learning.

While architectural sophistication increases model capability, it also introduces new challenges. Complex models often require large datasets, significant computational resources, and careful tuning to avoid overfitting. In advanced data science practice, model selection is therefore not solely a matter of performance metrics. It involves trade offs between accuracy, interpretability, computational cost, and operational feasibility.

Algorithmic intelligence extends beyond individual models to include how multiple models interact within a system. Ensemble methods combine predictions from multiple learners to improve robustness and reduce variance. Hybrid architectures integrate different learning paradigms to address diverse aspects of a problem. In intelligent decision systems, such combinations allow models to complement one another, balancing precision with stability.

Training strategies are another critical component of machine learning architecture. Batch learning assumes that training data is static and available upfront. Online and incremental learning approaches allow models to update continuously as new data arrives. In environments characterized by rapid change, incremental learning supports adaptability and reduces the risk of model obsolescence. Choosing the appropriate training strategy depends on data availability, system requirements, and tolerance for change.

Evaluation of machine learning models requires careful consideration in advanced systems. Standard metrics such as accuracy or error rates provide limited insight into long term behavior. Advanced evaluation practices assess model robustness, sensitivity to data drift, and performance under stress conditions. Cross validation, out of sample testing, and scenario based evaluation help identify weaknesses that may not appear in static benchmarks.

Interpretability remains a central concern as models grow more complex. Algorithmic intelligence that cannot be explained risks undermining trust and accountability. Advanced machine learning practice therefore incorporates techniques for model interpretation, such as feature attribution, surrogate modeling, and local explanation methods. These techniques enable stakeholders to understand how predictions are formed and to assess whether models align with domain knowledge and ethical expectations.

The deployment of machine learning models marks a critical transition from experimentation to operational intelligence. Models must integrate with data pipelines, application interfaces, and decision workflows. Deployment architectures determine how models are accessed, updated, and monitored. In production environments, issues such as latency, scalability, and fault tolerance shape architectural choices. Advanced systems often employ modular designs that allow models to evolve without disrupting surrounding components.

Monitoring and maintenance are essential for sustaining algorithmic intelligence over time. Machine learning models are sensitive to changes in data distributions, user behavior, and external conditions. Without monitoring, performance degradation can go unnoticed until negative outcomes occur. Advanced systems implement monitoring frameworks that track prediction quality, input characteristics, and usage patterns, enabling early detection of drift or failure.

Algorithmic intelligence also raises governance considerations. Decisions informed or executed by machine learning models must be accountable and auditable. Governance frameworks define how models are approved, documented, and reviewed. They establish standards for validation, version control, and retirement. In advanced data science environments, governance ensures that innovation remains aligned with organizational values and regulatory expectations.

Human involvement remains integral to machine learning systems despite increasing automation. Experts define objectives, select features, interpret outputs, and respond to unexpected behavior. Advanced architectures are designed to support this collaboration, providing interfaces that allow humans to interrogate models and intervene when necessary. This partnership enhances both system reliability and decision quality.

Machine learning architectures continue to evolve as research advances and new challenges emerge. Developments in self supervised learning, transfer learning, and federated learning promise to expand the reach of algorithmic intelligence while addressing constraints related to data availability and privacy. These innovations underscore the dynamic nature of the field and the need for continuous learning among practitioners.

2.1 Algorithmic Bias, Fairness, and Structural Risk in Machine Learning Systems

One critical area that warrants deeper exploration is the presence of algorithmic bias and its implications for intelligent decision systems. As machine learning models increasingly influence high impact decisions, issues of fairness, equity, and representational accuracy become central concerns rather than peripheral considerations. Advanced machine learning architectures can unintentionally encode and amplify existing biases present in data, leading to outcomes that disadvantage certain groups or distort decision quality.

Bias in machine learning often originates from historical data that reflects uneven social, economic, or institutional conditions. When such data is used to train models without careful scrutiny, the resulting systems may reproduce patterns that appear statistically valid but are ethically problematic. Advanced data science practice recognizes that bias is not solely a data problem or an algorithm problem. It is a systems problem that emerges from interactions between data collection processes, feature design, model objectives, and deployment contexts.

Fairness in machine learning therefore requires deliberate methodological choices. These include examining data sources for representational gaps, selecting features that minimize proxy discrimination, and defining performance metrics that capture more than aggregate accuracy. Advanced practitioners often employ fairness aware learning techniques that adjust model training to reduce disparate outcomes while preserving predictive value. These techniques reflect a broader understanding that performance and fairness must be balanced rather than treated as opposing goals.

Structural risk also arises when biased systems operate at scale. Automated decisions can propagate rapidly across digital platforms, amplifying the consequences of flawed assumptions. Advanced machine learning systems must therefore incorporate safeguards that detect and mitigate bias over time. Continuous evaluation, periodic audits, and feedback mechanisms play a crucial role in maintaining fairness as data and conditions evolve. In this context, algorithmic intelligence must be continuously examined rather than assumed to be neutral.

Addressing bias also requires organizational commitment. Technical solutions alone are insufficient if governance frameworks do not support accountability and corrective action. Advanced machine learning systems benefit from cross functional oversight involving technical experts, domain specialists, and ethical reviewers. This collaborative approach ensures that algorithmic decisions remain aligned with societal values and institutional responsibility.

2.2 Security, Robustness, and Adversarial Considerations in Learning Architectures

Another dimension of algorithmic intelligence that merits attention is security and robustness. Machine learning systems operate in environments where data inputs may be noisy, manipulated, or intentionally adversarial. Unlike traditional software systems, learning based architectures are particularly sensitive to subtle input changes that can significantly alter outputs. This vulnerability introduces new forms of risk that advanced data science must address.

Adversarial manipulation exploits the fact that models learn statistical patterns rather than semantic understanding. Carefully crafted inputs can cause models to misclassify or behave unpredictably, even when changes appear insignificant to human observers. In decision systems related to security, finance, or access control, such vulnerabilities can have serious consequences. Advanced machine learning practice therefore includes strategies to improve robustness against adversarial behavior.

Robustness strategies operate at multiple levels. At the data level, anomaly detection and validation mechanisms help identify suspicious inputs before they influence model behavior. At the model level, techniques such as regularization, adversarial training, and ensemble methods reduce sensitivity to perturbations. At the system level, layered defenses and redundancy limit the impact of individual model failures. These approaches reflect a systems oriented view of security that goes beyond protecting code or infrastructure alone.

Security considerations also extend to model intellectual property and data privacy. As machine learning models become valuable assets, they may be targeted for extraction or misuse. Advanced architectures increasingly incorporate privacy preserving techniques such as differential privacy and federated learning. These approaches allow models to learn from distributed data without exposing sensitive information, addressing both security and regulatory concerns.

Monitoring plays a crucial role in maintaining robustness over time. Threats evolve, and models trained on historical data may become vulnerable to new attack patterns. Advanced systems therefore implement continuous monitoring to detect shifts in input characteristics, prediction confidence, and outcome distributions. Early detection enables timely intervention and model updates, reducing exposure to emerging risks.

By addressing bias, fairness, security, and robustness as integral components of algorithmic intelligence, advanced machine learning architectures become more resilient and trustworthy. These considerations reinforce the idea that machine learning is not merely a technical tool, but a socio technical system embedded within broader environments of risk, responsibility, and accountability. As intelligent decision systems continue to expand their influence, attention to these dimensions becomes essential for sustaining confidence and long term value in data driven intelligence.

Chapter 3

Artificial Intelligence Strategies for Intelligent Decision Systems

Artificial intelligence has moved beyond experimental novelty to become a central force in how complex decisions are structured, executed, and evaluated within modern digital systems. While machine learning provides the mechanisms for pattern recognition and prediction, artificial intelligence strategies define how those mechanisms are organized into decision making frameworks that operate coherently and at scale. Intelligent decision systems are therefore not simply collections of models, but carefully designed architectures that translate analytical insight into action.

At the core of intelligent decision systems is the concept of decision orchestration. Rather than producing isolated predictions, AI driven systems coordinate multiple analytical components to support end to end decision processes. These components may include data ingestion pipelines, predictive models, optimization engines, rule based constraints, and feedback loops. The strategic challenge lies in aligning these elements so that decisions remain consistent, explainable, and adaptable across varying conditions.

One defining feature of AI strategies in decision systems is the shift from static logic to adaptive reasoning. Traditional decision support systems often relied on predefined rules that reflected historical assumptions. While such systems offered stability, they struggled to respond to change. AI driven decision systems, by contrast, are designed to learn from outcomes, update internal representations, and refine behavior over time. This adaptive capability enables systems to remain relevant in environments characterized by uncertainty and rapid evolution.

Intelligent decision systems also rely heavily on context awareness. Decisions are rarely optimal in isolation. They depend on timing, constraints, priorities, and external signals that shape their relevance. Advanced AI strategies incorporate contextual modeling to ensure that decisions reflect current conditions rather than abstract averages. Contextual features may include temporal patterns, environmental states, user behavior, or operational constraints. By embedding context into decision logic, systems achieve greater precision and situational relevance.

Another strategic dimension involves balancing automation with control. Fully automated decision systems can deliver speed and consistency, but they also raise concerns related to accountability and risk. Many intelligent systems therefore adopt semi autonomous strategies that combine automated analysis with human oversight. In such frameworks, AI systems generate recommendations or ranked options, while humans retain authority over final decisions. This balance preserves efficiency while maintaining responsibility and trust.

Optimization plays a central role in intelligent decision strategies. Beyond predicting outcomes, AI systems often seek to identify actions that maximize or minimize specific objectives under constraints. Optimization techniques such as linear programming, heuristic search, and reinforcement learning enable systems to evaluate trade offs and select actions that align with defined goals. In complex environments, optimization strategies must account for competing objectives, resource limitations, and uncertainty. Intelligent decision systems therefore integrate optimization as an ongoing process rather than a one time calculation.

Decision systems also benefit from modular design. Rather than embedding all logic within a single monolithic system, advanced AI strategies favor modular architectures where components can be updated independently. This approach supports scalability, experimentation, and risk management. Models can be retrained or replaced without disrupting surrounding processes, and decision logic can evolve as objectives change. Modularity enhances resilience and reduces dependency on any single analytical component.

Explainability remains a critical consideration in AI driven decision systems. As decisions influence high impact outcomes, stakeholders must understand not only what decisions were made, but why they were made. Advanced AI strategies incorporate explanation mechanisms that translate complex reasoning into accessible narratives. These explanations support auditability, regulatory compliance, and user trust. Without them, intelligent systems risk being perceived as opaque or unaccountable.

Feedback integration is another foundational strategy. Intelligent decision systems improve through exposure to outcomes and user interaction. Feedback loops allow systems to learn from successes and failures, adjusting decision logic accordingly. This learning process may be explicit, through labeled outcomes, or implicit, through behavioral signals. Effective feedback integration ensures that decision systems remain aligned with evolving objectives and real world dynamics.

AI strategies must also address decision latency and timing. In some contexts, decisions must be made in milliseconds. In others, deliberation and analysis are acceptable. Intelligent decision systems are designed with awareness of these temporal requirements. Real time systems prioritize speed and streamlined inference, while batch decision systems emphasize depth and accuracy. Strategic alignment between decision timing and system design is essential for effectiveness.

Risk management is deeply intertwined with intelligent decision strategies. Decisions informed by AI can introduce new forms of risk, particularly when systems operate autonomously or at scale. Advanced AI strategies incorporate risk assessment mechanisms that evaluate confidence, uncertainty, and potential impact. Decisions may be flagged for review when uncertainty exceeds acceptable thresholds. This approach allows systems to act decisively while avoiding overconfidence.

Governance structures shape how AI decision strategies are implemented and sustained. Clear policies define which decisions can be automated, how models are validated, and how exceptions are handled. Governance also establishes accountability for system outcomes. Intelligent decision systems that operate without governance frameworks often face resistance or misuse. Strategic alignment between technical design and governance ensures legitimacy and sustainability.

Human expertise remains central to AI driven decision systems. Domain knowledge informs objective definition, constraint selection, and interpretation of outcomes. Advanced AI strategies therefore emphasize collaboration between technical teams and domain experts. This collaboration ensures that decision logic reflects real world priorities and constraints rather than abstract optimization goals.

As AI capabilities continue to evolve, intelligent decision systems are becoming more autonomous, context aware, and adaptive. However, increased capability also increases responsibility. Decisions influenced by AI can shape markets, affect lives, and alter institutions. Advanced AI strategies must therefore prioritize not only performance, but also accountability, transparency, and resilience.

3.1 Cognitive Load Management and Decision Fatigue in AI Driven Systems

One area that has not yet been explored in depth is how intelligent decision systems affect human cognitive load. As AI driven systems become more capable, they often increase the volume, speed, and complexity of information presented to human decision makers. While this expansion is intended to improve decision quality, it can produce the opposite effect when not carefully managed. Cognitive overload and decision fatigue can reduce attention, increase error rates, and undermine trust in intelligent systems.

Advanced AI strategies must therefore consider not only what decisions are produced, but how those decisions are consumed by humans. Cognitive load management refers to the deliberate design of decision interfaces, information flow, and escalation logic to align with human capacity. Intelligent systems that overwhelm users with excessive alerts, complex explanations, or constant recommendations risk being ignored or misused. In contrast, systems that prioritize clarity, relevance, and timing enhance decision effectiveness.

Effective cognitive load management begins with prioritization. Not all analytical outputs require immediate attention. Advanced decision systems classify insights based on urgency, confidence, and potential impact. High risk or time sensitive decisions are surfaced prominently, while lower priority insights are deferred or summarized. This hierarchy allows decision makers to focus their attention where it matters most.

Another important strategy involves abstraction. Raw model outputs such as probabilities, scores, or multidimensional indicators may be meaningful to data scientists, but they can confuse operational users. Advanced AI systems translate complex analytics into simplified decision cues, such as ranked options, confidence bands, or scenario summaries. This abstraction does not reduce intelligence. Instead, it aligns system output with human decision processes.

Decision fatigue is also influenced by frequency. Systems that require constant human confirmation or intervention can exhaust users over time. Advanced AI strategies incorporate adaptive autonomy, where the level of automation adjusts based on system confidence and historical performance. When confidence is high and risk is low, systems may act autonomously. When uncertainty increases, human oversight is reintroduced. This adaptive approach preserves human energy for decisions that truly require judgment.

Training and familiarity further shape cognitive response. Decision systems that are poorly introduced or insufficiently explained increase mental effort. Advanced implementations include onboarding processes, decision simulations, and continuous learning resources that help users build mental models of system behavior. As familiarity increases, cognitive load decreases and trust improves.

Designing for cognitive alignment also requires acknowledging organizational context. Decision makers operate under time pressure, accountability requirements, and competing priorities. AI strategies that ignore these realities may deliver technically sound outputs that are practically unusable. Advanced intelligent decision systems therefore treat human attention as a scarce resource and design accordingly.

Case Study: Alert Saturation in an AI Driven Security Operations Platform

A large enterprise deployed an AI driven security operations platform designed to detect threats across network traffic, user behavior, and system logs. The platform integrated multiple machine learning models and generated real time alerts for potential security incidents. From a technical perspective, the system performed well. Detection rates improved and false negatives decreased significantly compared to legacy tools.

However, within months of deployment, security analysts began to experience alert fatigue. The system generated a high volume of notifications, many of which required manual review despite representing low risk events. Analysts reported difficulty prioritizing alerts and increasingly relied on heuristics rather than system recommendations. In some cases, critical alerts were delayed or overlooked due to cognitive overload.

An internal assessment revealed that while the system excelled at detection, it lacked effective cognitive load management. Alerts were presented without sufficient prioritization or contextual summarization. Analysts were required to interpret raw indicators and cross reference multiple data sources, increasing mental effort during already demanding workflows.

To address the issue, the organization restructured the decision strategy. Alerts were grouped into incident narratives that provided context, impact assessment, and recommended actions. Confidence thresholds were introduced to suppress low risk alerts or route them to automated response mechanisms. Human review was reserved for high impact or ambiguous cases. The interface was redesigned to highlight trends and escalation paths rather than isolated signals.

Following these changes, analyst efficiency improved and response times decreased. Trust in the system increased as users perceived it as a partner rather than a burden. The case demonstrates that intelligent decision systems must account for human cognitive limits. Without such consideration, increased intelligence can paradoxically reduce decision quality. When AI strategies are aligned with human attention and judgment, they deliver their intended value more effectively.

3.2 Governance, Accountability, and Escalation Logic in Intelligent Decision Systems

Another critical area that has not yet been examined in detail is how intelligent decision systems manage accountability. As artificial intelligence becomes more embedded in decision execution, questions arise around responsibility when outcomes fall short, decisions cause harm, or systems behave unexpectedly. Advanced AI strategies must therefore include clear governance structures and escalation logic that define when systems can act independently and when human intervention is required.

Accountability in intelligent decision systems begins with decision ownership. Every automated or AI assisted decision must have a clearly defined owner, even if the decision itself is generated by a system. This ownership ensures that outcomes can be reviewed, questioned, and improved over time. Without explicit accountability, organizations risk treating AI decisions as neutral outputs rather than consequential actions that require oversight.

Escalation logic plays a central role in maintaining accountability. Intelligent systems operate across varying levels of confidence and risk. Advanced AI strategies define thresholds that determine when decisions can be executed automatically and when they must be escalated for human review. These thresholds may be based on uncertainty measures, potential impact, regulatory sensitivity, or ethical considerations. Escalation logic ensures that high risk or ambiguous decisions receive appropriate scrutiny.

Governance frameworks also define how decisions are documented and audited. Intelligent systems should produce decision records that capture inputs, model versions, confidence levels, and contextual factors. This documentation supports post decision analysis and enables organizations to learn from outcomes. It also provides evidence for compliance and regulatory review, particularly in sectors where transparency is required.

Another governance consideration involves consistency across decision contexts. Intelligent systems often operate across departments or functions, each with different priorities and risk tolerances. Advanced AI strategies establish centralized governance principles that ensure consistent application of decision logic while allowing local adaptation where appropriate. This balance prevents fragmentation and reduces the likelihood of conflicting decisions.

Governance is not static. As systems evolve and new data becomes available, decision rules and escalation criteria must be reviewed and updated. Advanced decision systems incorporate governance review cycles that assess system performance, ethical implications, and alignment with organizational objectives. These reviews ensure that AI driven decisions remain appropriate over time.

Importantly, governance structures should not be viewed as barriers to innovation. When designed effectively, they provide clarity and confidence that enable organizations to deploy AI systems more widely. Clear rules around accountability and escalation reduce uncertainty for both technical teams and decision makers, fostering trust in intelligent systems.

Case Study: Accountability Breakdown in an Automated Resource Allocation System

A logistics organization implemented an AI driven resource allocation system to optimize vehicle deployment and delivery scheduling. The system combined demand forecasting models with optimization algorithms to assign resources dynamically across regions. Initial results showed improved efficiency and reduced delivery times, leading to rapid expansion of automated decision making.

Over time, however, operational issues emerged. Certain regions experienced persistent delays and resource shortages that were not adequately addressed by the system. Local managers reported that they had limited ability to override decisions or understand why resources were being allocated in specific ways. When service failures occurred, responsibility was unclear. Technical teams pointed to model logic, while operations teams deferred to system outputs.

An internal investigation revealed a lack of governance and escalation design. The system operated with broad autonomy, but decision ownership was not clearly defined. Escalation thresholds were absent, meaning that even high impact decisions were executed automatically without review. Decision logs captured technical data but did not provide accessible explanations for operational leaders.

To resolve the issue, the organization redesigned its AI decision strategy. Clear ownership was assigned for different decision categories, with designated managers responsible for outcomes. Escalation rules were introduced based on service impact and confidence levels, requiring human approval for high risk reallocations. Decision logs were enhanced to include summaries and rationale suitable for non technical stakeholders.

Following these changes, system performance stabilized and accountability improved. Managers regained confidence in the system and engaged more actively with its recommendations. The case highlights that intelligent decision systems must embed governance and escalation logic as core design elements. Without them, even highly optimized systems can undermine trust and effectiveness. When accountability is clearly defined, AI driven decisions become more reliable, transparent, and sustainable.

Chapter 4

Data Governance, Ethics, and Model Accountability

As data science and artificial intelligence systems become more deeply embedded in decision making processes, questions of governance and ethics move from abstract concerns to operational necessities. Intelligent systems increasingly influence outcomes related to finance, security, access to services, and resource distribution. In such contexts, the quality of decisions is measured not only by accuracy or efficiency, but also by fairness, transparency, and accountability. Data governance and ethical responsibility therefore form a central pillar of advanced intelligent decision systems.

Data governance refers to the structures, policies, and practices that determine how data is collected, managed, accessed, and used within an organization. In advanced data science environments, governance extends beyond data management to include model behavior, decision logic, and lifecycle oversight. Without strong governance, intelligent systems risk becoming opaque, inconsistent, or misaligned with organizational and societal expectations.

One of the foundational elements of data governance is clarity of ownership. Every dataset and analytical model must have clearly defined custodians responsible for its quality, use, and evolution. Ownership ensures accountability when issues arise and provides a point of authority for approving changes. In complex systems where data flows across multiple teams and platforms, the absence of clear ownership often leads to fragmented responsibility and weakened oversight.

Data quality management is another core governance concern. Advanced models are highly sensitive to the data they consume. Errors, inconsistencies, or biases in input data can propagate rapidly through intelligent systems, producing misleading or harmful outcomes. Effective governance frameworks establish standards for data validation, documentation, and lineage tracking. These practices ensure that data sources are understood, traceable, and suitable for their intended use.

Ethical considerations intersect closely with data governance. Ethical risks in data science often arise from seemingly technical decisions such as feature selection, labeling practices, or performance optimization. Advanced intelligent systems must therefore be designed with awareness of how such choices can influence outcomes across different populations. Ethical governance requires proactive identification of potential harm and deliberate mitigation strategies rather than reactive responses to failure.

Fairness is a central ethical concern in intelligent decision systems. Models trained on historical data may reflect existing inequalities or structural biases. When such models are deployed at scale, they can reinforce or amplify these patterns. Advanced data science practice addresses fairness through careful data analysis, bias testing, and the use of fairness aware modeling techniques. Governance frameworks define acceptable trade offs and establish processes for monitoring fairness over time.

Transparency plays a critical role in ethical accountability. Stakeholders affected by AI driven decisions often require explanations for how outcomes were reached. Advanced intelligent systems incorporate transparency mechanisms that provide insight into decision logic, contributing factors, and confidence levels. Transparency supports trust, enables contestability, and facilitates regulatory compliance. Without it, intelligent systems risk being perceived as arbitrary or unjust.

Model accountability extends beyond ethical intent to operational practice. Accountability requires that models can be audited, reviewed, and improved based on evidence. This includes maintaining detailed documentation of model objectives, training data, evaluation metrics, and deployment context. Version control and change management ensure that model updates are tracked and that decisions can be traced back to specific system states.

Lifecycle governance is another essential aspect of accountability. Models evolve as data changes and objectives shift. Governance frameworks define how models are monitored for performance degradation, bias emergence, or unintended consequences.

Regular reviews and retraining schedules help ensure that models remain aligned with current conditions. When models no longer meet standards, governance processes support responsible retirement rather than silent persistence.

Human oversight remains indispensable in ethical governance. While automated systems can process information at scale, ethical judgment often requires contextual understanding and moral reasoning. Advanced intelligent decision systems therefore integrate human review mechanisms, particularly for high impact or sensitive decisions. Governance structures specify when and how humans intervene, ensuring that ethical responsibility is shared rather than deferred to automation.

Regulatory alignment further shapes governance practices. Different jurisdictions impose varying requirements related to data protection, transparency, and accountability. Advanced data science systems must be designed with flexibility to comply with evolving regulatory landscapes. Governance frameworks provide a mechanism for translating regulatory obligations into technical and operational controls.

Ethical governance also involves cultural considerations. Organizations that treat ethics as a compliance exercise often struggle to embed responsible practices into daily operations. Advanced data science environments foster a culture where ethical reflection is part of system design and evaluation. Training, open discussion, and cross functional collaboration support this culture and encourage responsible innovation.

Conflicts between performance optimization and ethical constraints are inevitable. For example, maximizing efficiency may conflict with fairness goals, while automation may conflict with accountability. Advanced governance frameworks do not eliminate these tensions but provide structured processes for resolving them. Decision criteria, documentation, and stakeholder engagement help organizations navigate trade offs transparently and consistently.

The consequences of weak governance and ethical oversight can be significant. Intelligent systems that operate without accountability risk eroding trust, triggering regulatory action, or causing reputational harm. In contrast, systems designed with strong governance and ethical foundations are more resilient and sustainable. They adapt more effectively to change and maintain legitimacy even as they influence critical decisions.

4.1 Ethical Risk Anticipation and Proactive Harm Mitigation

One of the most underdeveloped aspects of data governance in intelligent systems is ethical risk anticipation. Many organizations approach ethics reactively, responding to failures only after harm has occurred. Advanced data science practice requires a proactive stance, where potential ethical risks are identified, assessed, and mitigated before systems are deployed at scale.

Ethical risk anticipation begins with recognizing that harm in intelligent systems is often indirect and cumulative. A single decision may appear benign, but repeated decisions influenced by the same model can produce systemic effects. These effects may include exclusion, unequal access, or reinforcement of structural disadvantage. Advanced governance frameworks therefore evaluate not only individual decisions, but aggregate outcomes over time.

Proactive harm mitigation involves embedding ethical checkpoints throughout the system lifecycle. During data collection, this includes evaluating representational balance and exclusion risks. During model development, it involves testing for disparate outcomes across different groups and scenarios. During deployment, it requires monitoring real world impact rather than relying solely on offline performance metrics.

Scenario analysis plays a critical role in ethical risk anticipation. Advanced teams simulate how systems behave under edge conditions, rare events, or adversarial contexts. These simulations help identify vulnerabilities that may not appear in standard testing. By anticipating how systems could fail ethically, organizations can design safeguards that prevent or reduce harm.

Ethical risk management also requires interdisciplinary collaboration. Technical teams alone may overlook social or contextual implications. Advanced governance structures involve legal experts, domain specialists, and ethics reviewers who contribute diverse perspectives. This collaborative approach strengthens risk identification and ensures that mitigation strategies are grounded in real world considerations.

Proactive ethics does not mean eliminating all risk. It means acknowledging uncertainty and preparing for it. Intelligent decision systems that incorporate ethical foresight are better equipped to adapt responsibly as conditions change. They also build trust with stakeholders who recognize that ethical responsibility has been taken seriously from the outset.

4.2 Accountability Frameworks and Traceability in Automated Decision Systems

Accountability in intelligent decision systems depends on the ability to trace outcomes back to their sources. Traceability refers to the capacity to reconstruct how a decision was made, which data and models were involved, and what contextual factors influenced the outcome. Without traceability, accountability becomes symbolic rather than operational.

Advanced accountability frameworks establish traceability as a core design requirement. This includes maintaining detailed records of data inputs, feature transformations, model versions, and decision logic. Decision logs must capture not only technical parameters, but also contextual metadata such as timing, confidence levels, and applicable constraints. These records enable meaningful review and learning.

Traceability supports multiple objectives. From a governance perspective, it enables internal audits and performance reviews. From a regulatory standpoint, it provides evidence of compliance with transparency and accountability requirements. From an operational standpoint, it supports debugging and system improvement when unexpected outcomes occur.

Automated decision systems often involve chains of interdependent components. A single outcome may reflect the interaction of several models, rules, and data sources. Advanced accountability frameworks address this complexity by documenting system architecture and dependencies. This documentation clarifies responsibility boundaries and prevents accountability gaps where no single owner can explain an outcome.

Human accountability remains essential even in highly automated systems. Advanced governance models assign responsibility for categories of decisions rather than individual outputs. This approach ensures that decision ownership is clear without requiring constant human intervention. Accountability becomes a shared responsibility supported by traceable systems rather than a barrier to automation.

Effective accountability frameworks also include processes for contestability. Stakeholders affected by decisions must have avenues to question outcomes and seek review. Traceable systems make such processes feasible by providing clear explanations and evidence. This capability strengthens legitimacy and reinforces ethical commitment.

By embedding traceability and accountability into system design, advanced data science environments move beyond symbolic ethics. They create practical mechanisms for responsibility that endure as systems scale and evolve. These frameworks ensure that intelligent decision systems remain subject to human values, oversight, and correction rather than operating as opaque authorities.

Chapter 5

Model Optimization, Performance, and Lifecycle Management

As intelligent systems mature and scale, the challenge facing data science teams shifts from building models to sustaining them. Initial performance gains achieved during development often diminish over time as data distributions change, objectives evolve, and operational constraints emerge. Model optimization and lifecycle management therefore become central to the long term success of advanced data science initiatives. Without disciplined approaches to performance tuning, monitoring, and renewal, even well designed models can quickly lose relevance or introduce unintended risk.

Model optimization begins with clarity of purpose. Optimization is not a generic pursuit of higher accuracy, but a targeted effort to align model behavior with specific decision objectives. Different contexts demand different optimization priorities. In some systems, minimizing false negatives may be critical. In others, stability, interpretability, or latency may matter more than marginal gains in predictive performance. Advanced data science practice requires explicit definition of optimization goals before model tuning begins.

Feature selection and representation play a foundational role in optimization. Models often underperform not because of algorithm choice, but because input features fail to capture relevant structure. Advanced optimization involves iterative feature analysis, testing alternative representations, and assessing how features contribute to performance across scenarios. This process benefits from both automated techniques and domain expertise. Human insight remains valuable in identifying meaningful signals that may not emerge through statistical correlation alone.

Hyperparameter tuning is another key optimization activity. Many machine learning models exhibit sensitivity to configuration choices such as learning rates, regularization strength, or network depth. Advanced teams employ systematic tuning strategies that balance exploration with computational efficiency. Grid search, randomized search, and adaptive optimization methods help identify configurations that perform consistently rather than exceptionally under narrow conditions. Robust performance across diverse inputs is often more valuable than peak performance on a single benchmark.

Optimization must also consider generalization. Models that perform extremely well on training or validation data may fail in real world settings if they overfit to historical patterns. Advanced data science emphasizes techniques that promote generalization, including regularization, cross validation, and stress testing under simulated conditions. These practices reduce the risk of brittle models that degrade quickly when exposed to change.

Performance evaluation extends beyond static metrics. Advanced systems assess performance longitudinally, tracking how models behave over time. Concept drift and data drift are common in dynamic environments. Changes in user behavior, market conditions, or data collection processes can alter input distributions and invalidate learned patterns. Lifecycle management frameworks include mechanisms to detect such shifts early and trigger investigation or retraining.

Monitoring infrastructure is therefore essential. Effective monitoring tracks both input characteristics and output behavior. Input monitoring identifies changes in data distributions, missing values, or anomalous patterns. Output monitoring evaluates prediction confidence, error rates, and decision outcomes. Together, these signals provide insight into system health and support proactive maintenance rather than reactive repair.

Lifecycle management also involves version control and documentation. Each model iteration represents a specific set of assumptions, data sources, and configuration choices. Advanced practice requires that these elements be documented clearly so that changes can be traced and evaluated. Versioning enables rollback when updates introduce unexpected issues and supports auditability in regulated environments. Documentation ensures continuity as teams evolve and personnel change.

Retraining strategies vary based on context. Some systems benefit from scheduled retraining at fixed intervals. Others require event driven retraining triggered by detected drift or performance decline. Advanced lifecycle management aligns retraining frequency with system volatility and risk tolerance. Over retraining can introduce instability, while under retraining allows degradation to persist. Finding the right balance is a strategic decision informed by monitoring data and operational constraints.

Optimization also intersects with resource management. Complex models often demand significant computational resources, which can limit scalability or increase cost. Advanced data science practice includes evaluation of model efficiency alongside performance. Techniques such as model compression, pruning, and approximation enable deployment of capable models within practical constraints. Optimization is therefore a multidimensional process that balances accuracy, efficiency, and sustainability.

Human oversight remains important throughout the lifecycle. Automated monitoring can surface issues, but human judgment is required to interpret signals and decide on corrective action. Advanced teams establish clear roles and processes for reviewing model performance, approving updates, and responding to incidents. This governance ensures that optimization efforts remain aligned with organizational objectives and ethical commitments.

Lifecycle management also includes responsible model retirement. Models that no longer meet performance or ethical standards should be decommissioned rather than left in place. Retirement decisions are often overlooked but are essential for maintaining system integrity. Advanced governance frameworks define criteria for retirement and ensure that downstream dependencies are addressed. This prevents outdated models from influencing decisions silently.

The relationship between optimization and governance is reciprocal. Governance frameworks define acceptable performance boundaries and risk thresholds. Optimization efforts operate within those boundaries. When objectives change or new risks emerge, governance processes guide adjustment. This alignment ensures that optimization does not pursue narrow technical gains at the expense of broader system responsibility.

Ultimately, model optimization and lifecycle management reflect a shift in how data science is practiced. Advanced systems are not built once and left unchanged. They are maintained, evaluated, and refined continuously. Performance is treated as a dynamic property rather than a static achievement. This perspective recognizes that intelligent systems exist within evolving environments and must adapt responsibly over time.

5.1 Performance Drift Detection and Adaptive Response Mechanisms

Performance drift represents one of the most subtle yet damaging risks to intelligent systems. Unlike abrupt system failures that trigger immediate alarms, drift unfolds gradually as underlying data patterns evolve. Changes in user behavior, external conditions, market dynamics, or data collection processes can all cause a model's learned assumptions to lose validity. Advanced data science recognizes drift not as an anomaly but as an expected condition in living systems.

Detecting drift requires deliberate instrumentation. Input drift occurs when the statistical properties of incoming data differ from those observed during training. Output drift manifests when prediction distributions change even if inputs appear stable. Outcome drift becomes evident when real world results no longer align with expected performance. Advanced systems monitor all three dimensions to build a comprehensive view of model health.

Statistical techniques such as distribution comparison, population stability metrics, and confidence variance tracking help identify early signals of degradation. However, raw detection is insufficient without contextual interpretation. Not every drift event warrants intervention. Some shifts reflect seasonal variation or benign adaptation. Advanced teams distinguish noise from meaningful change by correlating drift signals with business outcomes and system impact.

Adaptive response mechanisms define how systems react once drift is confirmed. Responses range from targeted retraining to feature redesign or objective recalibration. In some cases, drift reveals deeper changes in the environment that require strategic reconsideration rather than technical adjustment. Advanced lifecycle management therefore treats adaptation as a decision process rather than an automated reflex.

Importantly, response timing matters. Premature retraining can introduce instability and mask underlying issues. Delayed intervention allows degraded performance to persist. Effective systems define escalation thresholds that balance responsiveness with stability. These thresholds are informed by historical behavior, risk tolerance, and decision criticality.

Drift management also intersects with governance. Each adaptive action must be documented and reviewed to preserve accountability. By treating drift as a managed lifecycle event rather than a failure, advanced data science environments maintain resilience while preserving trust in intelligent systems.

5.2 Model Explainability and Performance Interpretability Over Time

Explainability is often emphasized at deployment but neglected during optimization and evolution. As models are retrained, features are updated, and objectives shift, internal reasoning patterns can change in ways that are difficult to detect without structured analysis. Advanced data science treats explainability as a continuous obligation rather than a one time requirement.

Performance interpretability focuses on understanding why a model behaves as it does and how that behavior evolves. Feature importance rankings that once appeared intuitive may gradually shift toward proxies that reflect noise or bias. Without continuous interpretability analysis, such changes can go unnoticed even as accuracy metrics remain stable.

Advanced systems employ longitudinal explainability methods that track how decision drivers evolve across model versions. Attribution analysis, sensitivity testing, and counterfactual evaluation provide insight into whether models rely on stable and meaningful signals. These techniques help teams detect emerging risks early and prevent optimization from drifting toward unintended behavior.

Interpretability also supports organizational learning. When stakeholders observe changes in model behavior, they require explanations that go beyond technical jargon. Clear interpretability narratives enable non-technical decision makers to understand system evolution and maintain confidence in analytical outputs. This transparency is essential for sustained adoption.

From a governance perspective, interpretability underpins auditability. Regulatory review, internal audits, and post incident investigations all depend on the ability to reconstruct decision logic. Advanced lifecycle frameworks embed interpretability artifacts into documentation and monitoring processes, ensuring that explanations remain available even as systems evolve.

Sustaining explainability over time requires intentional design. Models should be selected and optimized with interpretability constraints in mind, particularly in high impact contexts. Advanced data science acknowledges that maximum complexity is not always desirable. Instead, it prioritizes models whose reasoning can be examined, challenged, and improved responsibly.

5.3 Lifecycle Governance and Decision Threshold Management

Lifecycle governance provides the structural backbone that connects optimization, monitoring, and accountability. Without governance, performance management becomes reactive and fragmented. Advanced data science environments establish governance frameworks that define how decisions are made across the model lifecycle and who holds responsibility at each stage.

Decision thresholds play a central role in lifecycle governance. Thresholds determine when models are retrained, when alerts are escalated, and when human oversight is required. Poorly defined thresholds can cause instability by triggering excessive intervention or allowing degradation to persist unchecked. Advanced systems design thresholds that reflect risk sensitivity rather than arbitrary metrics.

Threshold management is inherently contextual. A minor accuracy decline may be acceptable in low impact recommendation systems but unacceptable in safety critical applications. Advanced governance frameworks therefore employ tiered thresholds that account for decision severity, uncertainty, and potential harm. This layered approach enables proportional responses rather than binary actions.

Governance also ensures that threshold changes are deliberate and transparent. As systems evolve, thresholds may require adjustment to reflect new objectives or conditions. Advanced environments document these changes, record rationale, and require approval through defined processes. This discipline prevents silent shifts in system behavior and preserves accountability.

Human oversight is integral to governance. Automated monitoring can identify signals, but humans determine significance and response. Governance frameworks clarify when human review is mandatory and how authority is exercised. This clarity protects both system integrity and organizational responsibility.

Lifecycle governance transforms optimization from a purely technical exercise into a managed institutional process. By formalizing how decisions are triggered, reviewed, and executed, advanced data science environments sustain intelligent systems that remain reliable, interpretable, and aligned with long term objectives.

Chapter 6

Analytical System Resilience and Operational Integrity

As intelligent systems become deeply embedded in operational environments, their ability to withstand disruption becomes as important as their ability to perform under normal conditions. Analytical system resilience refers to the capacity of data driven systems to continue functioning reliably when exposed to stress, uncertainty, or failure. Operational integrity ensures that decisions produced by these systems remain accurate, consistent, and trustworthy even when conditions deviate from expectation. Together, resilience and integrity define whether intelligent systems can be depended upon in real world contexts.

Modern digital systems operate within environments characterized by volatility. Data pipelines may experience outages, inputs may become noisy or incomplete, and external conditions may shift rapidly. Advanced data science acknowledges that such disruptions are not exceptional events but recurring features of complex systems. Resilient analytical systems are therefore designed with anticipation of failure rather than assumptions of stability.

One foundational element of resilience is fault tolerance. Analytical systems must be able to absorb component failures without collapsing entirely. This may involve redundant data sources, backup models, or failover mechanisms that preserve basic functionality when primary components become unavailable. Fault tolerance ensures continuity of decision support even when parts of the system are compromised.

Data resilience plays a critical role in operational integrity. Intelligent systems rely on continuous data flows, yet real world data is often incomplete or delayed. Advanced systems implement validation checks, fallback logic, and imputation strategies that allow analysis to proceed despite imperfect inputs. These measures prevent single point data issues from cascading into broader system failure.

Model robustness is another dimension of resilience. Analytical models must perform reasonably well across a range of conditions, not only those observed during training. Robust models exhibit stable behavior when inputs vary within plausible bounds and avoid extreme sensitivity to noise. Techniques such as regularization, ensemble modeling, and stress testing contribute to robustness by reducing dependence on fragile assumptions.

Operational integrity also depends on system observability. Teams must be able to see how analytical systems behave in real time. Observability includes logging, metrics, and alerts that provide insight into data quality, model performance, and decision outcomes. Without visibility, failures may remain undetected until significant damage occurs. Advanced systems prioritize observability as a core design principle rather than an afterthought.

Resilience extends beyond technical components to organizational processes. Incident response procedures define how teams react when systems behave unexpectedly. Clear roles, escalation paths, and communication protocols support rapid and coordinated response. Advanced data science environments integrate analytical incidents into broader operational risk management frameworks, ensuring that responses are consistent and accountable.

Graceful degradation is another key principle of resilient system design. When full functionality cannot be maintained, systems should degrade in predictable and controlled ways. For example, an intelligent system may switch from automated decision making to advisory mode when confidence falls below acceptable thresholds. Graceful degradation preserves safety and trust while allowing continued operation at reduced capability.

Security threats also test analytical resilience. Intelligent systems may be targeted through data manipulation, model exploitation, or infrastructure attacks. Resilient designs incorporate security controls such as input validation, access management, and monitoring for anomalous behavior. These measures help protect both data integrity and decision reliability.

Operational integrity requires alignment between analytical outputs and business processes. Decisions generated by intelligent systems must be integrated into workflows in ways that preserve accountability. Misalignment can lead to misuse, duplication, or neglect of analytical insight. Advanced systems ensure that decision pathways are clearly defined and supported by appropriate controls.

Change management further influences resilience. As systems evolve through updates and optimization, operational stability must be preserved. Poorly managed changes can introduce new vulnerabilities or disrupt established workflows. Advanced data science practice includes testing, staging, and rollback procedures that minimize risk during change. These practices support continuous improvement without compromising integrity.

Human factors remain central to resilience. While automated systems can detect and respond to certain issues, human judgment is essential for interpreting complex situations and making value based decisions. Advanced systems are designed to support human intervention rather than exclude it. Clear interfaces and decision summaries help humans understand system state and respond effectively.

Learning from failure is a hallmark of resilient systems. Post incident reviews analyze not only what failed but why safeguards were insufficient. These reviews inform system improvements and strengthen future resilience. Advanced organizations treat incidents as learning opportunities rather than solely as faults to be concealed.

Resilience also involves anticipating extreme scenarios. Stress testing and scenario planning expose systems to simulated disruptions, revealing weaknesses before they manifest in real operations. By preparing for adverse conditions, organizations reduce the likelihood of catastrophic failure and improve response readiness.

Analytical system resilience and operational integrity are not static properties. They evolve as systems grow in complexity and exposure. Maintaining resilience requires continuous investment in monitoring, governance, and skill development. It also requires cultural commitment to reliability and responsibility.

6.1 Stress Testing, Scenario Simulation, and Failure Anticipation in Analytical Systems

One important aspect of resilience that has not yet been explored in depth is the role of stress testing and scenario simulation. While monitoring and fault tolerance address issues as they arise, stress testing focuses on anticipating failure before it occurs. Advanced analytical systems cannot rely solely on historical performance to ensure future reliability. They must be deliberately exposed to extreme, unlikely, or adverse conditions in order to reveal hidden weaknesses.

Stress testing involves subjecting analytical systems to conditions beyond normal operating ranges. These conditions may include sudden spikes in data volume, severe data quality degradation, unexpected correlations, or rapid shifts in external signals. By observing how systems behave under stress, teams gain insight into their true limits. This process often uncovers vulnerabilities that remain invisible during routine operation.

Scenario simulation extends this concept by modeling plausible future states rather than purely technical extremes. Simulations may reflect economic shocks, operational disruptions, regulatory changes, or coordinated adversarial behavior. Advanced data science environments design scenarios collaboratively, drawing on domain expertise to ensure realism. These exercises help teams understand how analytical systems interact with broader organizational processes during periods of instability.

Failure anticipation is closely linked to stress testing. Rather than asking whether a system will fail, advanced teams ask how it is most likely to fail. This mindset shifts design priorities from prevention alone to preparation and recovery. Systems are evaluated not only on whether they produce correct outputs, but on how they behave when assumptions break down. Do they fail silently or visibly. Do they produce extreme outputs or degrade gracefully. Do they trigger alerts or continue operating incorrectly.

Stress testing also informs governance decisions. Results from simulations may reveal that certain automated decisions are too risky under specific conditions. In response, organizations may introduce additional safeguards, human review requirements, or alternative decision pathways. In this way, stress testing strengthens both technical resilience and decision governance.

Importantly, stress testing is not a one time activity. As systems evolve and new dependencies emerge, previously adequate safeguards may become insufficient. Advanced organizations incorporate stress testing into regular lifecycle reviews, treating it as an ongoing discipline rather than an occasional audit exercise.

Case Study: Stress Testing Failure in a Demand Forecasting and Inventory Optimization System

A national retail organization deployed an advanced demand forecasting and inventory optimization system to support automated replenishment across hundreds of locations. The system integrated historical sales data, seasonal patterns, promotional schedules, and external indicators to generate daily inventory recommendations. Under normal conditions, the system performed well, reducing stockouts and improving inventory turnover.

However, during an unexpected supply chain disruption, the system began producing erratic recommendations. Sudden delays in supplier deliveries combined with shifts in consumer demand created data patterns that differed significantly from historical norms. The forecasting model, trained primarily on stable conditions, failed to adjust quickly. As a result, some locations experienced excessive overstock while others faced severe shortages.

Post incident analysis revealed that the system had never been stress tested against extreme supply disruption scenarios. While the organization had tested model accuracy extensively under historical conditions, it had not simulated prolonged data gaps, delayed inputs, or rapid demand redistribution. The system lacked fallback logic to account for such disruptions and continued to generate recommendations with high confidence despite deteriorating data quality.

In response, the organization implemented a comprehensive stress testing program. Scenario simulations were developed to reflect supply interruptions, demand shocks, and data latency. During these simulations, system behavior was evaluated not only for accuracy but for stability and alerting behavior. Confidence thresholds were adjusted to trigger advisory mode during extreme uncertainty, requiring human review before execution.

The organization also introduced alternative decision pathways that relied on simpler heuristics when advanced models became unreliable. These safeguards ensured continuity of operations while preserving trust in the system. Following these changes, the system demonstrated improved resilience during subsequent disruptions.

6.2 Incident Response, Recovery Protocols, and Organizational Readiness

Another dimension of analytical system resilience that demands careful attention is incident response and recovery. While stress testing focuses on anticipating failure, incident response addresses what happens when failure actually occurs. No intelligent system is immune to disruption. Data pipelines break, models behave unexpectedly, and external events introduce conditions that exceed design assumptions. The difference between resilient and fragile systems often lies in how organizations respond when things go wrong.

Incident response in advanced data science environments extends beyond technical troubleshooting. It involves coordinated action across data science teams, engineering, operations, and leadership.

Clear response protocols define how incidents are detected, who is notified, and what actions are taken to stabilize systems. Without such protocols, response becomes ad hoc, delayed, and inconsistent, increasing the impact of failure.

Early detection is the first pillar of effective incident response. Monitoring systems must be capable of identifying anomalies in data quality, model behavior, and decision outcomes. Alerts should be meaningful rather than excessive, guiding attention to issues that require intervention. Advanced systems distinguish between minor deviations and critical incidents, ensuring that response efforts are proportional to risk.

Once an incident is detected, containment becomes the priority. Containment strategies aim to limit the spread of erroneous decisions and prevent further harm. This may involve disabling automated execution, reverting to previous model versions, or switching to manual or heuristic based processes. Effective containment preserves operational continuity while reducing exposure to incorrect or unstable outputs.

Recovery protocols define how systems are restored to normal operation. Recovery involves diagnosing root causes, correcting data or model issues, and validating fixes before redeployment. Advanced organizations maintain recovery playbooks that outline steps for different incident types. These playbooks reduce uncertainty during high pressure situations and support consistent response across teams.

Communication is a critical component of incident response. Stakeholders affected by system behavior must be informed in a timely and transparent manner. Clear communication builds trust and enables coordinated decision making. Advanced data science environments establish communication channels and messaging guidelines to ensure that information flows effectively during incidents.

Organizational readiness also influences recovery success. Teams must be trained to execute response protocols and understand system dependencies. Regular drills and incident simulations help build familiarity and confidence. These exercises reveal gaps in preparedness and provide opportunities for improvement before real incidents occur.

Post incident review is essential for learning and improvement. Rather than assigning blame, advanced organizations conduct structured reviews that examine technical, procedural, and organizational factors. These reviews inform updates to models, monitoring systems, and governance frameworks. By learning from incidents, organizations strengthen resilience over time.

Incident response also intersects with accountability and ethics. When intelligent systems influence critical decisions, failures may have significant consequences. Advanced response frameworks include mechanisms for assessing impact, providing remediation, and addressing affected parties. This reinforces ethical responsibility and supports long term trust.

Case Study: Recovery Breakdown in an Automated Pricing Intelligence System

An e commerce company implemented an AI driven pricing intelligence system to adjust product prices dynamically based on demand signals, competitor activity, and inventory levels. The system operated with high autonomy and updated prices multiple times per day. Initial results showed increased revenue and improved inventory management.

During a major promotional period, the system began generating erratic price fluctuations. A combination of incomplete competitor data and delayed inventory updates caused the model to misinterpret market conditions. Prices dropped sharply for certain products and spiked for others, leading to customer complaints and revenue loss.

Although monitoring systems detected unusual behavior, response was delayed. There was no clear protocol for disabling automated pricing, and decision ownership was ambiguous. Teams debated responsibility while the system continued operating. By the time manual intervention occurred, the incident had already caused significant disruption.

Following the incident, the organization conducted a comprehensive review. It identified gaps in incident detection thresholds, unclear escalation paths, and insufficient recovery planning. In response, the company implemented a structured incident response framework. Automated execution was tied to confidence and data quality checks. Clear authority was assigned for disabling systems during anomalies. Recovery playbooks were developed for common failure scenarios.

The organization also introduced regular incident simulations to test readiness. These exercises improved coordination and reduced response times. Subsequent incidents were contained quickly, minimizing impact.

Chapter 7

Intelligent Decision Systems in High-Risk and Regulated Environments

As intelligent decision systems increasingly influence critical outcomes, their deployment in high-risk and regulated environments demands heightened discipline, scrutiny, and responsibility. Sectors such as finance, healthcare, energy, public administration, and national security operate under conditions where errors carry severe consequences. In these domains, analytical intelligence must meet standards that extend beyond performance, incorporating reliability, transparency, and compliance as foundational requirements rather than optional enhancements.

High-risk environments are defined by the scale of impact associated with decisions. A flawed recommendation in a low-stakes system may result in minor inefficiency. In contrast, errors in regulated or safety-critical contexts can lead to financial loss, legal liability, physical harm, or erosion of public trust. Intelligent systems deployed in such environments must therefore be designed with conservative assumptions and robust safeguards. Advanced data science practice recognizes that the cost of failure shapes system design priorities.

Regulatory frameworks play a central role in shaping intelligent decision systems in these contexts. Regulations often specify requirements related to data protection, auditability, explainability, and accountability. Rather than viewing regulation as a constraint on innovation, advanced practitioners treat it as a design input. Systems are architected to produce evidence, explanations, and controls that align with regulatory expectations. This proactive alignment reduces friction during audits and supports sustainable deployment.

One defining challenge in regulated environments is balancing automation with control. While automation offers efficiency and consistency, excessive autonomy can conflict with regulatory mandates that require human judgment and accountability. Intelligent decision systems therefore adopt layered decision strategies. Automated components handle routine or low-risk tasks, while higher impact decisions trigger human review or approval. This structure preserves efficiency while maintaining compliance and responsibility.

Documentation becomes especially important in regulated contexts. Intelligent systems must generate records that explain how decisions were reached, which data sources were used, and which models were involved. These records support regulatory review, internal audits, and dispute resolution. Advanced systems treat documentation as a live artifact rather than static paperwork, updating it continuously as models evolve.

Validation standards are also more stringent in high-risk environments. Models must demonstrate not only accuracy but stability, fairness, and robustness under diverse conditions. Validation processes often include independent review, stress testing, and scenario analysis. These practices help ensure that intelligent systems behave predictably even when exposed to edge cases or adverse conditions.

Ethical considerations intersect strongly with regulation in these settings. Decisions influenced by intelligent systems may affect access to credit, healthcare treatment, employment opportunities, or public services. Advanced data science practice acknowledges that ethical responsibility cannot be delegated entirely to compliance functions. Ethical reasoning must inform system objectives, feature selection, and evaluation criteria. This integration helps prevent harm that may technically comply with rules but violate broader societal expectations.

Cross functional collaboration is essential in regulated environments. Data scientists, engineers, legal experts, risk managers, and domain specialists must work together to design and govern intelligent systems. Each group brings perspectives that shape system behavior and risk profile. Advanced organizations establish governance forums where these stakeholders collaborate throughout the system lifecycle rather than only during approval stages.

Operational constraints further influence system design in high-risk contexts. Latency requirements, data access limitations, and security controls may restrict model complexity or deployment options. Advanced practitioners adapt architectures to function effectively within these constraints rather than pursuing maximal sophistication. Simpler models with clear behavior may be preferred over complex architectures that are difficult to explain or control.

Human training and readiness also determine success. Decision makers who interact with intelligent systems must understand system capabilities and limitations. Overreliance on automation can lead to complacency, while excessive skepticism can undermine value. Advanced deployment strategies include training programs that help users interpret outputs critically and exercise informed judgment.

Incident response takes on heightened importance in regulated environments. Failures must be detected quickly and addressed transparently. Regulatory obligations may require notification, remediation, or reporting within defined timeframes. Intelligent systems must therefore be integrated into broader compliance and risk management processes. Advanced organizations plan for incidents as part of system design rather than treating them as exceptional events.

Change management is equally critical. Updates to models or decision logic may require revalidation or regulatory approval. Advanced lifecycle management frameworks track changes meticulously and ensure that updates do not introduce unapproved behavior. This discipline supports continuous improvement without compromising compliance.

The deployment of intelligent decision systems in high-risk and regulated environments underscores a central theme of this book. Advanced data science is not only about capability. It is about responsibility. Systems that influence critical outcomes must be designed to withstand scrutiny, operate transparently, and respect human values. Innovation in these contexts succeeds when intelligence is matched by governance and foresight.

7.1 Regulatory Alignment as a Design Principle Rather Than a Compliance Layer

One of the most critical mistakes organizations make in regulated environments is treating regulation as an external constraint applied after system development. Advanced intelligent decision systems reverse this logic by embedding regulatory alignment directly into system design. Rather than retrofitting controls, these systems are built from the outset to generate transparency, traceability, and audit readiness.

Regulatory alignment begins with understanding regulatory intent rather than focusing narrowly on rule interpretation. Many regulations are designed to ensure fairness, accountability, data protection, and human oversight. When intelligent systems are architected with these principles in mind, compliance becomes a natural outcome rather than a burdensome obligation. This approach reduces friction between technical teams and compliance functions.

Designing for alignment influences architectural choices. Data pipelines must preserve lineage and consent context. Models must support explanation and review. Decision logic must be structured in ways that allow intervention and override. These design decisions may constrain certain forms of automation, but they also create systems that are more robust, defensible, and trusted.

Advanced organizations establish regulatory design reviews early in the system lifecycle. These reviews assess whether proposed architectures can satisfy documentation, validation, and accountability requirements before development proceeds. This proactive engagement prevents costly redesigns and delays during deployment.

By treating regulation as a design input rather than an obstacle, intelligent systems achieve greater longevity. They adapt more easily to evolving regulatory landscapes and maintain legitimacy in environments where scrutiny is continuous.

7.2 Human Authority, Override Rights, and Decision Accountability

In high risk and regulated environments, human authority must remain clearly defined even when intelligent systems operate autonomously. Advanced decision systems do not eliminate human responsibility. Instead, they redistribute it in ways that preserve accountability while leveraging computational intelligence.

Human authority is expressed through override rights. Override mechanisms allow designated individuals to intervene when system outputs conflict with contextual knowledge, ethical judgment, or regulatory requirements. These mechanisms must be clearly specified and operationally accessible. If overrides are difficult to execute or discouraged culturally, they become symbolic rather than functional.

Decision accountability requires clarity around who is responsible for outcomes. In regulated contexts, accountability cannot be diffused across systems, teams, or vendors. Advanced frameworks assign responsibility at the decision category level. Individuals or roles are accountable for approving automated logic, reviewing escalations, and addressing failures.

Training plays a critical role in preserving human authority. Decision makers must understand when to trust system recommendations and when to challenge them. Overreliance on automation can lead to abdication of responsibility, while distrust can undermine value. Advanced organizations invest in education that builds calibrated trust rather than blind acceptance.

Human authority also supports ethical governance. Automated decisions may technically comply with rules while producing outcomes that conflict with broader values. Human oversight provides a moral checkpoint that cannot be fully automated. By preserving clear authority and accountability, intelligent systems remain aligned with both regulatory and societal expectations.

7.3 Auditability, Evidence Generation, and Long Term Institutional Trust

Auditability is a defining requirement for intelligent decision systems in regulated environments. Audits are not exceptional events but recurring mechanisms through which institutions demonstrate responsibility. Advanced systems are designed to generate evidence continuously rather than reconstruct it retrospectively.

Evidence generation involves capturing decision inputs, model versions, confidence measures, and contextual constraints. This information must be stored in structured and accessible formats that support review by technical and non technical stakeholders. Advanced systems automate much of this process to reduce manual burden and ensure consistency.

Auditability supports more than regulatory compliance. It strengthens internal governance by enabling performance review, risk assessment, and learning. When decisions can be examined and explained, organizations gain insight into system behavior and areas for improvement.

Long term institutional trust depends on transparency and reliability. Stakeholders are more likely to accept AI driven decisions when systems can explain themselves and demonstrate consistent adherence to rules and values. Auditability reinforces this trust by making accountability visible rather than assumed.

Advanced data science environments treat audits as opportunities for improvement rather than threats. Findings inform system refinement, governance enhancement, and training initiatives. This continuous feedback loop strengthens resilience and credibility over time.

By embedding auditability and evidence generation into system design, intelligent decision systems earn the confidence required to operate in high risk and regulated environments. Trust becomes an outcome of disciplined design rather than a matter of reputation alone.

Chapter 8

Emerging Innovations in Intelligent Decision Systems

The field of intelligent decision systems is evolving at a pace that continually reshapes how data driven intelligence is conceived, designed, and applied. Advances in data science and artificial intelligence are not merely refining existing methods. They are introducing new paradigms that challenge assumptions about data availability, system autonomy, governance, and human interaction. Emerging innovations expand both the capability and the responsibility of intelligent systems, making foresight and adaptability essential qualities for practitioners.

One significant trend shaping the future of intelligent decision systems is the move toward learning with limited supervision. Traditional machine learning approaches rely heavily on large labeled datasets, which are expensive and time consuming to produce. Emerging methods such as self supervised and weakly supervised learning reduce this dependence by extracting structure directly from raw data. These approaches enable systems to learn more efficiently and adapt to new domains where labeled data is scarce.

Transfer learning represents another important innovation. By leveraging knowledge learned in one context and applying it to another, systems can achieve strong performance with fewer resources. Transfer learning supports faster deployment and continuous improvement, particularly in environments where conditions evolve rapidly. Intelligent decision systems that incorporate transfer mechanisms can respond more effectively to change while preserving stability.

Federated learning introduces a novel approach to data collaboration. Rather than centralizing data, federated systems train models across distributed data sources while keeping raw data local. This approach addresses privacy concerns and regulatory constraints related to data sharing. In regulated environments, federated learning enables collective intelligence without compromising data protection obligations. It represents a shift toward cooperative intelligence that respects institutional boundaries.

Another area of innovation involves causal inference and decision focused learning. While many machine learning models identify correlations, emerging approaches seek to understand cause and effect relationships. Causal modeling enables decision systems to evaluate the impact of interventions rather than merely predicting outcomes. This capability is particularly valuable in policy design, healthcare, and risk management, where decisions alter the environment itself.

Decision focused learning aligns model objectives directly with decision outcomes. Rather than optimizing predictive accuracy alone, these methods optimize for the quality of decisions made using model outputs. This shift reframes performance evaluation and encourages closer integration between modeling and operational objectives. Intelligent decision systems built on decision focused principles are better aligned with real world goals.

Explainable artificial intelligence continues to advance as a critical innovation area. New methods aim to provide more faithful and stable explanations for complex models. These approaches improve transparency and support accountability in high impact systems. As regulatory and ethical expectations grow, explainability innovations will play a central role in sustaining trust.

Human centered AI represents another emerging direction. Innovations in interface design, interaction models, and decision support aim to enhance collaboration between humans and intelligent systems. Rather than replacing human judgment, these systems augment it by providing structured insight and adaptive guidance. Human centered design acknowledges that decision quality depends on how information is presented and interpreted.

Autonomous system coordination is also gaining prominence. As multiple intelligent systems interact within shared environments, coordination mechanisms become essential. Innovations in multi agent learning and decentralized decision making support cooperation among systems while managing conflict and competition. These approaches are particularly relevant in logistics, infrastructure management, and distributed operations.

Security and resilience innovations continue to shape the future of intelligent decision systems. Techniques for robust learning, adversarial defense, and secure deployment are evolving in response to growing threats. Emerging approaches focus on detecting manipulation, preserving integrity, and maintaining performance under attack. These innovations strengthen system resilience in increasingly hostile environments.

Ethical innovation is another important frontier. New frameworks and tools aim to operationalize ethical principles rather than treat them as abstract guidelines. Automated fairness assessment, impact evaluation, and governance tooling enable organizations to manage ethical risk proactively. These innovations reflect a broader recognition that ethics must be embedded into system design and operation.

The convergence of intelligent decision systems with emerging technologies further expands innovation potential. Integration with Internet of Things platforms, edge computing, and real time analytics enables decisions to be made closer to where data is generated. This reduces latency and supports responsiveness in dynamic environments. However, it also introduces new governance and security challenges that must be addressed.

As innovation accelerates, the role of strategic foresight becomes increasingly important. Not every new technique is appropriate for every context. Advanced practitioners evaluate innovations through the lens of risk, governance, and long term sustainability. Responsible adoption requires balancing experimentation with discipline.

8.1 Decentralized Intelligence and Edge Based Decision Architectures

One of the most transformative innovations in intelligent decision systems is the shift toward decentralized intelligence. Traditional architectures rely on centralized data collection and processing, which can introduce latency, scalability limits, and governance challenges. Emerging edge based decision architectures distribute intelligence closer to where data is generated, enabling faster and more context aware decisions.

Edge based systems process data locally on devices or within constrained environments rather than transmitting all data to centralized servers. This approach supports real time responsiveness in settings such as industrial automation, smart infrastructure, healthcare monitoring, and connected transportation. Decisions can be made with minimal delay, improving system effectiveness in time sensitive contexts.

Decentralized intelligence also reshapes governance and privacy considerations. By limiting data movement, edge architectures reduce exposure to data breaches and regulatory risk. Sensitive data can remain within its original context while contributing to collective intelligence through aggregated or abstracted insights. This aligns well with evolving data protection expectations and sovereignty requirements.

However, decentralization introduces new complexity. Coordinating decision logic across distributed nodes requires careful design to ensure consistency and alignment with organizational objectives. Advanced decision systems address this challenge through hierarchical control structures and synchronization mechanisms that balance local autonomy with global oversight.

Edge based decision architectures also influence model design. Lightweight models optimized for constrained environments may replace highly complex centralized models. This tradeoff favors efficiency, interpretability, and reliability over maximal predictive power. Advanced practitioners recognize that decision quality often depends more on timeliness and robustness than on marginal accuracy gains.

As decentralized intelligence becomes more prevalent, organizations must rethink how decision authority, monitoring, and accountability are distributed. Edge based systems represent not just a technical shift, but a structural transformation in how intelligent decisions are produced and governed.

8.2 Strategic Foresight and Responsible Innovation in Intelligent Systems

As intelligent decision systems evolve rapidly, strategic foresight becomes an essential capability. Emerging innovations offer powerful tools, but unchecked adoption can introduce long term risk. Responsible innovation requires the ability to anticipate how new technologies may reshape decision processes, governance structures, and societal expectations.

Strategic foresight involves examining trends, uncertainties, and potential futures to inform present day design choices. In the context of intelligent systems, this means evaluating how advances such as autonomous decision making, causal modeling, and decentralized intelligence may alter accountability and control. Advanced organizations incorporate foresight into system planning rather than treating innovation as reactive experimentation.

Responsible innovation balances exploration with restraint. Not every technically feasible capability should be deployed. Advanced data science practice includes ethical and institutional impact assessment alongside technical evaluation. This ensures that innovation aligns with organizational values and public trust rather than pursuing novelty for its own sake.

Foresight also supports adaptability. Systems designed with future evolution in mind are more resilient to change. Modular architectures, flexible governance frameworks, and continuous learning processes enable organizations to integrate new innovations without destabilizing existing operations. This adaptability is especially important as regulatory and societal expectations continue to evolve.

Education and leadership play a central role in responsible innovation. Decision makers must understand both the promise and limitations of emerging technologies. Advanced organizations invest in developing leaders who can evaluate innovation critically and guide adoption responsibly. This leadership ensures that intelligent systems evolve in ways that strengthen rather than undermine institutional integrity.

By embedding strategic foresight into innovation processes, organizations position themselves as thoughtful stewards of intelligent decision systems. Innovation becomes a deliberate and accountable journey rather than an uncontrolled race. In this way, emerging technologies contribute to long term value, resilience, and trust within the digital frontier.

Chapter 9

The Future of Data Governance and Intelligent Decision Stewardship

As intelligent decision systems continue to expand in scope and influence, the future of data science will be shaped less by technical capability alone and more by how intelligence is governed, stewarded, and trusted over time. Data governance is no longer a background function focused on access control and compliance. It is becoming a strategic discipline that determines whether intelligent systems can operate responsibly within complex social, economic, and institutional environments.

The increasing autonomy of intelligent systems amplifies the importance of stewardship. Decisions informed by data science now affect markets, public services, security operations, and individual opportunities at scale. In this context, stewardship refers to the responsibility of organizations and professionals to guide how intelligence is created, deployed, and evolved. It emphasizes long term impact rather than short term performance gains.

Future data governance frameworks will need to move beyond static rule sets. Traditional governance models often rely on fixed policies that struggle to keep pace with rapidly evolving systems. Intelligent decision systems learn, adapt, and interact in ways that challenge rigid oversight structures. As a result, governance must become adaptive, capable of evolving alongside the systems it regulates.

One defining feature of future governance is continuous oversight. Rather than approving systems once and assuming ongoing compliance, governance bodies will monitor system behavior throughout its lifecycle. Performance, fairness, robustness, and ethical impact will be assessed continuously. This shift reflects an understanding that risk emerges over time and must be managed dynamically.

Transparency will also evolve as a governance expectation. Stakeholders increasingly demand insight into how decisions are made and how systems change. Future governance frameworks will require intelligent systems to provide accessible explanations tailored to different audiences, from technical reviewers to affected individuals. Transparency will serve not only accountability, but also learning and trust building.

The role of data ownership will become more nuanced. As data flows across organizational and geographic boundaries, questions of ownership, consent, and responsibility grow more complex. Future governance models will emphasize stewardship over possession. Organizations will be expected to demonstrate responsible data handling regardless of where data originates or how it is shared.

Institutional trust will depend heavily on how governance is enacted in practice. Governance that exists only on paper fails to influence real outcomes. Future frameworks will integrate governance mechanisms directly into technical systems through automated controls, audit trails, and policy enforcement. This integration ensures that governance is operational rather than symbolic.

Ethical governance will also mature. Instead of reacting to ethical failures after harm occurs, future stewardship models will prioritize anticipation and prevention. Impact assessments, ethical simulations, and stakeholder engagement will become standard components of system design. These practices recognize that ethical responsibility must be proactive to be effective.

Interdisciplinary collaboration will shape the future of governance. Data scientists alone cannot anticipate all consequences of intelligent systems. Governance bodies will increasingly include legal experts, social scientists, ethicists, and domain specialists. This diversity of perspective strengthens oversight and helps align technical innovation with societal expectations.

Global coordination presents another governance challenge. Intelligent systems often operate across borders, while regulations remain largely national. Future governance approaches will need to reconcile differing legal regimes and cultural values. International standards and shared principles may provide a foundation for alignment, even as local adaptation remains necessary.

Education and professional development will influence governance outcomes. As intelligent systems become more complex, the gap between technical experts and decision makers can widen. Future stewardship models will emphasize shared understanding, ensuring that leaders and regulators possess sufficient literacy to engage meaningfully with data driven systems.

Accountability mechanisms will also evolve. Rather than focusing solely on individual responsibility, future frameworks will address collective accountability across teams and institutions. This approach reflects the reality that intelligent systems are built and maintained collaboratively. Clear role definition and shared responsibility structures will be essential.

Public engagement will play a growing role in governance. As intelligent decision systems affect broader populations, legitimacy will depend on transparency and inclusion. Mechanisms for feedback, contestation, and redress will strengthen trust and ensure that governance reflects public values rather than purely institutional priorities.

The future of data governance is therefore inseparable from the future of intelligent decision stewardship. Governance will no longer be an administrative function operating at the margins of innovation. It will be a central design principle that shapes how intelligence is produced and applied.

9.1 Adaptive Governance Models for Learning and Evolving Systems

One of the defining challenges for the future of data governance is the rise of systems that learn and evolve continuously. Traditional governance frameworks were designed for static systems with predictable behavior. Intelligent decision systems challenge this assumption by updating models, adapting to new data, and altering decision logic over time. Future governance must therefore be adaptive rather than fixed.

Adaptive governance models focus on oversight mechanisms that evolve alongside intelligent systems. Rather than relying solely on pre deployment approval, these models emphasize continuous evaluation. Performance, fairness, robustness, and ethical alignment are assessed at regular intervals using predefined indicators. When deviations occur, governance processes trigger review and corrective action.

This approach requires close integration between governance and technical infrastructure. Monitoring tools feed governance dashboards that provide real time insight into system behavior. Automated policy checks enforce constraints related to data use, decision authority, and risk thresholds. Human governance bodies retain final authority, but they are supported by continuous evidence rather than periodic reports.

Adaptive governance also allows for contextual flexibility. Different decision environments require different oversight intensity. Low risk systems may operate with minimal intervention, while high impact systems are subject to tighter review cycles. By adjusting governance rigor based on risk and impact, organizations avoid one size fits all control models that either over constrain innovation or leave critical systems under supervised.

In the future, adaptive governance will be essential for maintaining legitimacy as intelligent systems grow more autonomous. It acknowledges that learning systems cannot be governed effectively through static rules alone. Instead, governance itself must become a learning process grounded in observation, feedback, and refinement.

9.2 Institutional Accountability and Collective Responsibility Frameworks

As intelligent decision systems become more complex, accountability can no longer be assigned to a single individual or function. These systems are designed, trained, deployed, and maintained by teams that span technical, operational, and leadership roles. Future stewardship therefore requires a shift from individual accountability to collective responsibility.

Collective accountability frameworks define how responsibility is shared across roles while preserving clarity. Rather than asking who built the model, these frameworks ask who approved its use, who monitors its behavior, and who responds when outcomes fall short. Accountability is distributed across the lifecycle rather than concentrated at development.

Clear role definition is central to this approach. Data stewards oversee data quality and consent. Model owners are responsible for performance and alignment with objectives. Decision owners are accountable for how outputs are used in practice. Governance committees provide oversight and escalation pathways. This structure ensures that no critical responsibility is left undefined.

Collective accountability also supports ethical governance. When responsibility is shared transparently, ethical concerns are more likely to surface early. Teams feel empowered to raise issues rather than deferring responsibility to the system or to leadership alone. This cultural shift strengthens stewardship and reduces the risk of silent failure.

In the future, institutions that succeed with intelligent systems will be those that formalize collective accountability rather than relying on informal norms. Stewardship becomes an organizational capability rather than an individual trait.

9.3 Public Trust, Transparency, and the Social License to Operate

The long term success of intelligent decision systems depends not only on internal governance but on public trust. As these systems influence broader populations, they require a social license to operate. This license is granted through transparency, accountability, and meaningful engagement with those affected by decisions.

Future governance models will treat transparency as a communication practice rather than a technical disclosure. Providing raw technical explanations is insufficient. Intelligent systems must explain themselves in ways that are understandable and relevant to different audiences. Affected individuals require clarity about how decisions impact them and how those decisions can be questioned.

Mechanisms for contestation and redress will become central to stewardship. People affected by automated decisions must have pathways to challenge outcomes and seek review. These processes reinforce legitimacy and signal that intelligent systems remain subject to human values and institutional responsibility.

Public trust also depends on consistency between stated values and operational behavior. Governance frameworks must demonstrate that ethical commitments are enforced in practice. This includes acting decisively when systems cause harm and communicating transparently about corrective measures.

Engagement with external stakeholders will increasingly shape governance. Civil society groups, regulators, and independent reviewers contribute perspectives that internal teams may overlook. Incorporating these voices strengthens oversight and aligns intelligent systems with societal expectations.

In the future, intelligent decision systems will operate not only within technical and legal boundaries but within a social context defined by trust. Organizations that recognize and respect this reality will be better positioned to sustain innovation and legitimacy in an increasingly data driven world.

Chapter 10

Guardianship, Leadership, and the Responsible Future of Intelligent Systems

The evolution of data science and intelligent decision systems has brought society to a defining moment. Analytical intelligence now shapes decisions that influence economies, institutions, and individual lives. What began as a technical discipline has matured into a force that carries ethical, social, and strategic implications. At this stage of development, the central question is no longer whether intelligent systems can be built, but how they should be guided, governed, and led.

Throughout this book, a consistent theme has emerged. Intelligent systems do not exist independently of human intent. They reflect the values, assumptions, and priorities of those who design and deploy them. As these systems grow more capable, the responsibility of their stewards grows accordingly. Guardianship becomes the defining role of modern data science professionals, extending beyond technical expertise into leadership and ethical judgment.

Guardianship in this context refers to the deliberate protection of decision integrity over time. It requires a commitment to ensuring that intelligent systems remain aligned with their intended purpose even as conditions change. Guardians anticipate risk, question assumptions, and act when systems drift away from acceptable boundaries. This role demands vigilance rather than complacency and reflection rather than blind reliance on automation.

Leadership is inseparable from guardianship. Advanced data science environments require leaders who understand both the promise and the limits of intelligent systems. Technical leadership alone is insufficient. Leaders must be capable of integrating analytical insight with organizational values, regulatory expectations, and societal impact. They must foster cultures where evidence informs decisions but does not replace accountability.

One of the most important leadership responsibilities is setting ethical direction. Ethical behavior in intelligent systems does not emerge automatically from technical correctness. It is shaped by the objectives defined, the tradeoffs accepted, and the safeguards implemented. Leaders establish these boundaries through policy, governance, and example. When ethical considerations are treated as secondary, systems may deliver efficiency at the cost of trust.

Guardianship also requires humility. Intelligent systems operate within complex environments that resist complete prediction. Unexpected behavior, edge cases, and unintended consequences are inevitable. Responsible leaders acknowledge uncertainty and design systems that can be questioned, corrected, and improved.

Humility encourages continuous learning and prevents overconfidence in automated outcomes.

Human centered design remains a cornerstone of responsible intelligence. While automation increases speed and scale, human judgment provides context, empathy, and moral reasoning. Guardians ensure that intelligent systems support human decision making rather than displacing it entirely. This balance preserves agency and reinforces accountability, particularly in high impact contexts.

Institutional resilience depends on this balance. Organizations that treat intelligent systems as infallible authorities often struggle when failures occur. In contrast, those that view systems as tools within a broader decision ecosystem respond more effectively to disruption. Guardianship involves preparing institutions to engage critically with intelligence rather than surrendering control to it.

Education and mentorship play a vital role in sustaining guardianship. As new practitioners enter the field, they inherit not only technical tools but also responsibility. Advanced data science education must therefore emphasize governance, ethics, and leadership alongside algorithms and infrastructure. Mentorship reinforces these values and builds continuity across generations of practitioners.

Collaboration across disciplines strengthens guardianship further. Complex decision systems benefit from perspectives beyond data science. Legal experts, domain specialists, ethicists, and operational leaders contribute insights that shape more resilient and legitimate systems. Guardians encourage this collaboration and resist siloed decision making.

The global nature of intelligent systems adds another layer of responsibility. Decisions informed by data science often cross borders and cultures. Guardians must remain sensitive to differing norms, expectations, and regulatory environments. Responsible leadership recognizes that intelligence deployed in one context may have unintended effects in another.

Looking ahead, the future of intelligent decision systems will be defined not only by innovation but by trust. Trust is earned through transparency, accountability, and demonstrated care over time. Guardianship ensures that trust is maintained even as systems evolve and scale.

10.1 Leadership Under Uncertainty and the Ethics of Decision Authority

One area that has not yet been examined in depth is how leadership functions when intelligent systems operate under uncertainty. Advanced intelligent decision systems often produce outputs with varying degrees of confidence. They may recommend actions based on incomplete data, probabilistic forecasts, or rapidly changing conditions. In such situations, leadership is tested not by certainty, but by judgment.

Leadership under uncertainty requires the ability to interpret intelligence without surrendering authority to it. Intelligent systems can surface patterns and probabilities, but they cannot fully account for contextual nuance, moral consequence, or long term institutional impact. Guardianship therefore involves knowing when to rely on system recommendations and when to pause, question, or override them.

Ethics of decision authority become especially relevant in these moments. When outcomes carry significant consequences, leaders must ask not only what the system suggests, but whether acting on that suggestion aligns with organizational values and societal responsibility. Delegating authority to intelligent systems does not absolve leaders of accountability. Instead, it demands greater clarity about who holds final responsibility and why.

Advanced leadership frameworks emphasize decision framing. Rather than treating system outputs as answers, leaders treat them as inputs into a broader deliberative process. Confidence scores, scenario ranges, and uncertainty indicators inform judgment rather than dictate it. This approach preserves human agency and ensures that responsibility remains visible and intentional.

Leadership under uncertainty also requires courage. There are moments when intelligent systems recommend actions that are technically justified but ethically questionable or socially sensitive. Guardianship demands the willingness to challenge intelligence in favor of principled restraint. This restraint protects institutional credibility and reinforces trust among stakeholders.

Importantly, leaders must model this behavior. When teams observe leadership engaging critically with intelligent systems, they learn that questioning automation is not resistance but responsibility. This cultural signal is essential for sustaining ethical intelligence at scale.

Case Study: Ethical Override in an AI Driven Public Resource Allocation System

A metropolitan public administration introduced an AI driven system to optimize allocation of emergency response resources across districts. The system analyzed historical incident data, population density, traffic patterns, and response times to recommend dynamic redistribution of emergency units. Early simulations showed improved efficiency and reduced average response times.

During a period of heightened public tension following a series of unrelated events, the system recommended reallocating resources away from several low incident districts toward higher risk zones. Technically, the recommendation was justified by data patterns. However, leadership recognized that the affected districts had limited access to alternative services and were experiencing increased public anxiety.

Relying solely on the system recommendation risked reinforcing perceptions of neglect and undermining public trust. Senior leaders chose to override the automated decision partially, maintaining baseline coverage in vulnerable districts while implementing targeted adjustments elsewhere. This decision resulted in slightly lower optimization metrics but preserved public confidence and equity.

Following the incident, leadership initiated a review of decision authority policies. The system was updated to include social vulnerability indicators and to flag recommendations with potential equity implications for mandatory human review. Clear guidelines were established outlining when ethical considerations should supersede optimization goals.

10.2 Cultivating a Culture of Responsible Intelligence and Long Term Stewardship

Beyond individual leadership decisions, the sustainability of intelligent systems depends on organizational culture. Even the most carefully designed governance frameworks and ethical policies will fail if they are not reinforced by shared values and daily practice. Cultivating a culture of responsible intelligence means embedding stewardship into how teams think, work, and make decisions over time.

Responsible intelligence culture begins with how success is defined. Organizations that reward speed, efficiency, or short term performance at all costs often create incentives that undermine ethical judgment. Advanced stewardship reframes success to include reliability, fairness, transparency, and long term impact. When these qualities are recognized and rewarded, teams internalize responsibility rather than treating it as an external constraint.

Communication plays a critical role in shaping culture. Leaders who speak openly about uncertainty, risk, and ethical tradeoffs signal that thoughtful judgment is valued. This openness reduces fear around questioning intelligent systems and encourages constructive dialogue. Teams become more willing to raise concerns when they believe such actions will be supported rather than penalized.

Training and continuous learning reinforce cultural alignment. Responsible intelligence requires more than technical competence. Practitioners must understand governance principles, ethical reasoning, and system impact. Advanced organizations integrate these topics into onboarding, professional development, and leadership training. This shared knowledge base ensures that responsibility is distributed rather than concentrated among a few specialists.

Psychological safety is another essential component. Teams must feel safe to challenge assumptions, report anomalies, and question system behavior. Intelligent systems often fail silently when concerns are suppressed. A culture that encourages inquiry and dissent strengthens resilience and prevents small issues from becoming systemic failures.

Long term stewardship also requires continuity. Intelligent systems outlive individual contributors and leadership tenures. Cultural norms provide stability as personnel change. When stewardship values are embedded institutionally, responsibility persists even as teams evolve. This continuity protects systems from degradation driven by turnover or shifting priorities.

Importantly, culture shapes how organizations respond to failure. In responsible intelligence environments, failures are treated as learning opportunities rather than sources of blame. Post incident reviews focus on system improvement and cultural reinforcement. This approach encourages transparency and continuous improvement.

Case Study: Cultural Breakdown and Recovery in an Enterprise Risk Analytics Program

A multinational organization launched an enterprise wide risk analytics program to support strategic planning and operational decision making. The system integrated predictive models across finance, supply chain, and compliance functions. Technically, the program was well designed and supported by strong infrastructure.

However, over time, cultural issues emerged. Teams were incentivized to demonstrate performance improvements quickly, leading to aggressive automation and reduced human oversight. Analysts who raised concerns about model assumptions or ethical implications were often dismissed as slowing progress. As a result, early warning signals were ignored.

Eventually, the system produced recommendations that contributed to a significant operational misstep. While technically defensible, the decision failed to account for regulatory nuance and stakeholder impact. The incident exposed a culture that prioritized metrics over judgment and efficiency over responsibility.

In response, leadership initiated a cultural reset. Incentive structures were revised to value risk awareness and responsible escalation. Training programs emphasized stewardship and ethical reasoning. Leaders publicly acknowledged the cultural failures that contributed to the incident and committed to change.

Over time, the organization rebuilt trust internally and externally. Teams became more engaged in governance processes and more willing to challenge intelligent systems constructively. The analytics program recovered and evolved into a more balanced and resilient capability.

Reviews

1. Dr. Lanre Oyekan| Associate Professor of Data Analytics, Crestview School of Computing, Nigeria

Guardians of the Digital Frontier stands out as a deeply researched and carefully structured contribution to advanced data science literature. The book demonstrates a clear appreciation for the realities of deploying intelligent systems within complex environments. Its emphasis on analytical integrity, system resilience, and long term reliability reflects a mature understanding of data science as both a technical and institutional discipline.

2. Ms. Rukayat Ajibola | Lead Analytics Strategist, Novatrix Digital Finance Solutions, Nigeria

This work addresses critical gaps often overlooked in applied data science practice. The author goes beyond model performance to explore how intelligent decision systems must be governed, optimized, and sustained over time. The discussion of model lifecycle management and decision accountability is particularly relevant for organizations operating data driven platforms at scale.

3. Engr. Sadiq Musa | Chief Data Infrastructure Architect, Ironclad Systems Technologies, Nigeria

One of the most compelling aspects of this book is its systems level perspective. It recognizes that intelligent decision systems depend heavily on infrastructure stability, data governance, and disciplined execution. The chapters focused on analytical resilience and operational integrity provide insights that are both research grounded and directly applicable to enterprise environments.

4. Dr. Aisha Mohammed | Senior Research Scientist, Ethos Intelligence Research Group, Nigeria

This book makes an important scholarly contribution to discussions on responsibility and trust in intelligent systems. The treatment of transparency, governance, and human oversight is integrated seamlessly into the technical discourse. Rather than separating ethics from engineering, the author presents them as inseparable components of sustainable data driven intelligence.

5. Mr. Kunle Fasina | Head of Decision Systems Advisory, VectorPoint Technology Consulting, Nigeria

Guardians of the Digital Frontier offers a thoughtful examination of how data science must evolve as systems grow more complex and influential. The author avoids exaggerated innovation claims and instead delivers a disciplined, research supported framework for intelligent system design. The focus on leadership, stewardship, and long term impact makes this book especially valuable for senior practitioners and technical decision makers.

References

Bishop, C. M. (2006). Pattern recognition and machine learning. Springer.

Breiman, L. (2001). Random forests. Machine Learning, 45(1), 5–32. https://doi.org/10.1023/A:1010933404324

Brynjolfsson, E., & McAfee, A. (2017). Machine, platform, crowd: Harnessing our digital future. W. W. Norton & Company.

Doshi-Velez, F., & Kim, B. (2017). Towards a rigorous science of interpretable machine learning. arXiv preprint arXiv:1702.08608. https://arxiv.org/abs/1702.08608

European Commission High-Level Expert Group on Artificial Intelligence. (2019). Ethics guidelines for trustworthy AI. European Commission. https://digital-strategy.ec.europa.eu

Goodfellow, I., Bengio, Y., & Courville, A. (2016). Deep learning. MIT Press.

Hardt, M., Price, E., & Srebro, N. (2016). Equality of opportunity in supervised learning. Advances in Neural Information Processing Systems, 29, 3315–3323.

Jordan, M. I., & Mitchell, T. M. (2015). Machine learning: Trends, perspectives, and prospects. Science, 349(6245), 255–260. https://doi.org/10.1126/science.aaa8415

Kearns, M., & Roth, A. (2019). The ethical algorithm: The science of socially aware algorithm design. Oxford University Press.

Kroll, J. A., Huey, J., Barocas, S., Felten, E. W., Reidenberg, J. R., Robinson, D. G., & Yu, H. (2017). Accountable algorithms. University of Pennsylvania Law Review, 165(3), 633–705.

Mitchell, M. (2019). Artificial intelligence: A guide for thinking humans. Farrar, Straus and Giroux.

Molnar, C. (2019). Interpretable machine learning. Lulu.com. https://christophm.github.io/interpretable-ml-book/

Pearl, J., & Mackenzie, D. (2018). The book of why: The new science of cause and effect. Basic Books.

Ribeiro, M. T., Singh, S., & Guestrin, C. (2016). "Why should I trust you?" Explaining the predictions of any classifier. Proceedings of the 22nd ACM SIGKDD International Conference on Knowledge Discovery and Data Mining, 1135–1144. https://doi.org/10.1145/2939672.2939778

Sculley, D., Holt, G., Golovin, D., Davydov, E., Phillips, T., Ebner, D., Chaudhary, V., Young, M., Crespo, J. F., & Dennison, D. (2015). Hidden technical debt in machine learning systems. Advances in Neural Information Processing Systems, 28, 2503–2511.

Shalev-Shwartz, S., & Ben-David, S. (2014). Understanding machine learning: From theory to algorithms. Cambridge University Press.

Taleb, N. N. (2012). Antifragile: Things that gain from disorder. Random House.

Varian, H. R. (2019). Artificial intelligence, economics, and industrial organization. AEA Papers and Proceedings, 109, 399–404. https://doi.org/10.1257/pandp.20191051

Wachter, S., Mittelstadt, B., & Russell, C. (2017). Counterfactual explanations without opening the black box. Harvard Journal of Law & Technology, 31(2), 841–887.

Zhang, Y., & Chen, X. (2020). Explainable AI in deep learning. IEEE Access, 8, 136769–136787. https://doi.org/10.1109/ACCESS.2020.3011697

www.ingramcontent.com/pod-product-compliance
Lightning Source LLC
Chambersburg PA
CBHW021215250926
51852CB00006B/13